THE BOOK OF ART is designed as an introduction to the visual arts: painting, drawing and sculpture. It provides a comprehensive survey, in ten volumes, of one of the most creative aspects of human effort, especially organized for the reader who does not have an extensive knowledge of the history of art.

Textual material prepared by experts in each school of art presents a detailed background of information. But, since art must be seen to be understood and appreciated, the essence of each volume lies in the color plates and the large number of black-and-white illustrations.

The first volume discusses the origins of the visual arts in the western world. The following five volumes are devoted to national schools of painting, extending roughly from the early Renaissance up to the mid-19th century. The two succeeding volumes cut across national divisions and deal first with the Impressionists and Post-Impressionists and then with 20th-century art. The ninth volume deals with the rich art of China and Japan.

The final volume, *How to Look at Art*, is designed to aid the reader in developing an appreciative understanding of the entire field of art. It discusses art of all schools and periods, with relevant illustrations, both in color and black-and-white, throughout the text. The same volume concludes with an illustrated glossary of art terms and a comprehensive index covering all ten volumes.

THE BOOK OF ART

A Pictorial Encyclopedia of Painting, Drawing, and Sculpture

VOLUME 4

GERMAN AND SPANISH ART TO 1900

THE BOOK OF ART

A Pictorial Encyclopedia of Painting, Drawing, and Sculpture

GERMAN AND SPANISH ART TO 1900

Edited by

Dr. Horst Vey

Wallraf-Richartz-Museum, Cologne

and

Dr. Xavier de Salas

Deputy Director, Museo del Prado, Madrid

Grolier
INCORPORATED

NEW YORK   MONTREAL   MEXICO CITY   SYDNEY

HOW TO USE THIS BOOK

To obtain the maximum information and interest from this series it is necessary to understand its basic plan. With the exception of the first volume and the last two volumes, which are more general in their scope, each of the other seven volumes is arranged as follows:

First, a historical Introduction sets out the main lines of development within the school or period, with special reference to the major artists and the major works of art.

This is followed by a biographical section outlining the life and work of every major artist and important minor artists. The Biographies run in alphabetical order according to the name by which each artist is most generally known, whether it be surname, or Christian name (as for example LEONARDO da Vinci), or nickname (as TINTORETTO). With each biography is given a cross-reference to the page or pages on which he is represented in the plates sections which follow; a monochrome reproduction of one or more of his other works; and (where possible) a self-portrait or portrait of the artist and a specimen of his signature.

Next follow the sections of Color Plates, Drawings, and Sculpture. Each of these sections is arranged in chronological order according to the date of the artist's birth, though in a few cases minor adjustments to this order have been made for the sake of comparison or design. To illustrate painting techniques, particularly of frescoes and large easel paintings, some color plates show a detail rather than the whole work; but the use of such a detail is indicated in the caption, and a monochrome illustration of the whole work is normally given with the artist's biography; in such cases the size given in the caption refers to the whole painting. The location of every work of art is included in its caption. Every effort has been made to include also the size, medium, and date of each work represented in the plates, though this has not always been possible since not every museum has such information available for all the items in its collection. The reader will also appreciate that the precise dating of many works of art is the subject of scholarly controversy; however, no dates have been included here unless they have the authority of qualified experts and art historians.

A final section, entitled Influences and Developments, rounds off the period by drawing together the main ideas and characteristics of schools and styles, and by exploring the internal and external influences that have made their impact on the development of the arts during the period concerned.

This particular volume is divided into two parts, covering the art of Germany and Spain respectively up to the end of the 19th century.

A list of basic reference books for further reading appears on pages 16 and 160. Books containing material of special interest concerning an individual artist are listed at the end of the relevant biography.

To avoid repetitive explanation of basic technical terms such as *genre*, *chiaroscuro*, *baroque*, etc., an illustrated Glossary is provided in the volume entitled *How to Look at Art*. Also in that volume is an Index listing every artist mentioned throughout the series.

Taken as a whole, the series thus provides a comprehensive, carefully integrated, and highly informative survey of the achievement and significance of Western Art from its origins to the present day.

NOTE.—The terminal dates in the titles of some of the volumes are inevitably approximate. One volume will sometimes overlap with another. Some artists mentioned under French Art, for example, are also represented under the Impressionists, and the Post-Impressionists merge imperceptibly with the Moderns. In the ever-continuous process of Art it is difficult to contain schools or periods within precise boundaries.

Copyright (©) 1965 by Grolier Incorporated
First published 1965. Second Impression 1966. Third Impression 1967. Fourth Impression 1967.
Library of Congress Catalog Card Number: 65-10350

Designed and produced by George Rainbird Ltd., London
PRINTED IN ITALY by Amilcare Pizzi S.p.A., Milan

Contents

LIST OF COLOR PLATES

ACKNOWLEDGMENTS

The publishers and producers wish to express their gratitude to all the museums, art galleries, collectors, photographers, and agencies who have courteously assisted them in obtaining the material for the illustrations reproduced in this volume. They would especially like to thank the following:

German Art

Albertina, Vienna
Albertina Graphische Sammlung, Vienna
Alte Pinakothek, Munich
Ampliaciones y Reproducciones Mas, Barcelona
The Armory, Augsburg
Bayerisches Landesamt für Denkmalpflege, Munich
Bayerisches Nationalmuseum, Munich
Bayerische Staatsbibliothek, Munich
Bayerischen Staatsgemäldesammlungen, Munich
Bildarchiv Foto, Marburg
Bildstelle und Denkmalsarchiv, Nuremberg
Foto Blasczyk, Düsseldorf
Joachim Blauel, Munich
E. G. Bührle Collection, Zürich
Colorphoto Hans Hinz SWB, Basel
The Courtauld Institute of Art, London
Deutsche Fotothek, Dresden
Evangelisches Pfarramt, Bad Wildungen
Fratelli Alinari, S.A. (I.D.E.A.), Florence
Fürstenbergische Galerie, Donaueschingen
Gemäldegalerie, Dresden
Gemäldesammlung der Benediktinerabtei, Vienna
Gemeinschaft Bildender Künstler, Vienna
Germanisches Nationalmuseum, Nuremberg
Photographie Giraudon, Paris
Goethemuseum, Frankfurt-am-Main
Leo Gundermann, Würtzburg
Herzog Anton Ulrich-Museum, Brunswick
Herzog-August Bibliothek, Wolfenbüttel
Hessisches Landesmuseum, Darmstadt
Historisches Archiv, Cologne
Historisches Museum, Frankfurt-am-Main
Holle Verlag GmbH, Baden-Baden
Kunsthalle, Bremen
Kunsthalle, Hamburg
Kunsthistorisches Museum, Vienna
Kunstmuseum, Basel
Kunstmuseum, Bern
Kunstmuseum, Darmstadt
Kunstsammlungen, Maximilienmuseum, Augsburg
Kupferstichkabinett, West Berlin
Kupferstichkabinett, Dresden
Landesmuseum, Hanover
Landesmuseum, Innsbruck
Lichtbildwerkstatt Ann Bredol-Lepper, Aachen
The Louvre, Paris
Mainfränkisches Museum, Würzburg
Mauritshuis, The Hague
Musée d'Art et d'Histoire, Geneva
Musée Royal des Beaux-Arts, Antwerp
Musée des Beaux-Arts, Reims
Musée d'Unterlinden, Colmar
Museum der Bildenden Künste, Leipzig

Museum für Kunst und Gewerbe, Hamburg
Museum für Kunst and Kulturgeschichte, Dortmund
The Trustees of the National Gallery, London
The National Museum, Helsinki
Neue Pinakothek, Munich
Niedersächsisches Landesmuseum, Hanover
Niedersächsisches Landesverwaltungsamt, Brunswick
Österreichische Galerie, Vienna
Photo-Wehmeyer, Hildesheim
Porzellansammlung, Dresden
Prado, Madrid
Farbenfotografie Gerhard Reinhold, Leipzig
Rheinisches Bildarchiv, Cologne
Rijksmuseum, Amsterdam
Messrs. Karl Robert, Königstein im Taunus
The Royal Collection, London, by gracious permission of
    Her Majesty the Queen
Édouard Rutter and Son, Luxembourg
Schlossmuseum, Weimar
Staatliches Amt für Denkmalpflege, Stuttgart
Staatliche Graphische Sammlung, Munich
Staatliche Kunsthalle, Karlsruhe
Staatliche Kunstsammlungen, Dresden
Staatliche Kunstsammlungen, Stuttgart
Staatliche Münzsammlung, Munich
Staatliche Museen, Berlin
Staatliches Museum für Völkerkunde, Munich
Staatsgalerie, Stuttgart
Städelsches Kunstinstitut, Frankfurt-am-Main
Stadtarchiv, Cologne
Stadtbibliothek (Stadtarchiv), Trier
Stadtbibliothek, Ulm
Städtische Galerie, Augsburg
Städtische Kunsthalle, Mannheim
Städtische Kunstsammlung, Augsburg
Städtische Kunstsammlung, Nuremberg
Städtische Sammlungen für Kunst and Kulturgeschichte, Ulm
Statens Museum for Kunst, Copenhagen
Suermondt Museum, Aachen
Universitätsbibliothek, Erlangen
Universitätsbibliothek, Würzburg
The Vatican Gallery, Rome
Verwaltung der Staatlichen Schlösser und Gärten,
    West Berlin
The Victoria and Albert Museum (Crown Copyright), London
The Wallraf-Richartz-Museum, Cologne

Spanish Art

Ampliaciones y Reproducciones Mas, Barcelona
Anderson Photos, Rome
T. & R. Annan and Sons Ltd., Glasgow
Apsley House, London
The Art Museum, Princeton University, Princeton, N.J.
Bell, Howarth Ltd., London
Biblioteca de Palacio, Madrid
Biblioteca Nacional, Madrid
The Trustees of the British Museum, London
The Business Exchange, Palma de Mallorca
Centro de Estudios Historicos, Madrid
Cofradia de los Navarros, Madrid
The Courtauld Institute of Art, London
The Courtauld Institute Galleries, University of London
Deutsche Fotothek, Dresden

Acknowledgments continued

Doria Pamphili Palace, Rome
The Escorial, Madrid
Duke of Fernán Nuñez Collection, Madrid
John R. Freeman and Co., London
Gemäldegalerie, Dresden
Photographie Giraudon, Paris
The Hispanic Society of America, New York
Hospital de la Caridad, Seville
Hospital de Tavera, Toledo, Spain
Junta de Comercio, Avila
Junta de Comercio, Burgos
Junta de Comercio, Cordova
Junta de Comercio, Gerona
Junta de Comercio, Granada
Junta de Comercio, León
Junta de Comercio, Madrid
Junta de Comercio, Manzanares
Junta de Comercio, Salamanca
Junta de Comercio, Santiago de Compostela
Junta de Comercio, Segovia
Junta de Comercio, Seville
Junta de Comercio, Toledo, Spain
Junta de Comercio, Valencia
Kunsthistorisches Museum, Vienna
The Library of Congress, Washington, D. C.
The Louvre, Paris
Mrs. Maxwell MacDonald, Pollok House, Glasgow
Magyar Szépmüvészeti Muzeum, Budapest
The Mansell Collection, London
The Metropolitan Museum of Art, New York
Monasterio de Descalzes Reales, Madrid
Monasterio de San Isidoro del Campo, Santiponce
Museo Arqueológico Provincial, Burgos
Museo de Bellas Artes, Barcelona
Museo de Bellas Artes, Valencia
Museo Diocesano, Salamanca
Museo Lázaro, Madrid
Museo Nacional de Arte Moderno, Madrid
Museo Nacional de Escultura Religiosa, Valladolid
Museo Nazionale, Naples
Museo Provincial de Bellas Artes, Seville
Museo Provincial de Bellas Artes, Cadiz
Museo Provincial de Bellas Artes, Vitoria
Museo Salzillo, Murcia
Museo San Carlos, Valencia
The Museum and Art Gallery, São Paolo, Brazil
The Museum of Fine Arts, Boston, Mass.
Museum of Fine Arts of Catalonia, Barcelona
The Trustees of the National Gallery, London
The National Gallery of Art, Washington, D. C.
The National Gallery of Scotland, Edinburgh
Nether Pollock Ltd., Glasgow
Palacio Nacional, Madrid
Palais des Beaux-Arts, Lille
Patrimonio Nacional, Palacio de Oriente, Madrid
The Philadelphia Museum of Art, Philadelphia, Pa.
The Prado, Madrid
Gonzal Mighel Ojeda, Archivo Fotografico de Arte, Burgos
Real Academia de Bellas Artes de San Jorge, Barcelona
Real Academia de San Fernando, Madrid
Mr. Hugo P. Rudinger, Berkeley, California
Scala, Instituto Fotografico Editoriale, Florence
Tom Scott, Edinburgh

Staatliche Kunstsammlungen, Dresden
Staatliche Museen, Berlin
Statens Museum for Kunst, Copenhagen
The Uffizi Gallery, Florence
The Victoria and Albert Museum (Crown Copyright), London
The Trustees of the Wallace Collection, London

ABBREVIATIONS

attrib.	attributed, attribution
et al.	and elsewhere
in.	inches
S.	Saint, Sacred (Italian and Spanish)
SS.	Santissimo, Santissima (Italian)
St.	Saint (English and German)
St. or Ste.	Saint (French)
Acad.	Academy, Academia
Accad.	Accademia
B-A.	Beaux-Arts
B. A.	Bellas Artes
Bibl.	Biblioteca, Bibliothek, Bibliothèque
B. M.	British Museum, London
Cath.	Cathedral
Coll.	Collection
Gal.	Galerie
Gall.	Galleria, Gallery
Gemäldegal.	Gemäldegalerie
Inst.	Institut, Institute, Instituto
Kunsthist.	Kunsthistorisches
Kunstinst.	Kunstinstitut
Kunstmus.	Kunstmuseum
Kunstsamm.	Kunstsammlung
Landesmus.	Landesmuseum
Met. Mus.	Metropolitan Museum of Art, New York
Mus.	Musée, Museen, Museo, Museu, Museum
Nac.	Nacional
Nat.	National, Nationale
Naz.	Nazionale
N. G.	National Gallery, London; National Gallery of Art, Washington, D. C.
Pin.	Pinacoteca, Pinakothek
Rijksmus.	Rijksmuseum, Amsterdam
Samm.	Sammlung
Schlossmus.	Schlossmuseum
Staatl.	Staatliche
Staatsgal.	Staatsgalerie
V. and A.	Victoria and Albert Museum, London

GERMAN ART
TO 1900

Edited, with an Introduction, by

Dr. Horst Vey

Wallraf-Richartz-Museum, Cologne

Introduction

German Art to 1900

German art is much neglected by the English-speaking amateur. One of the reasons for this is that, during the great periods of collecting, the Gothic and northern Renaissance styles, in which the best achievements of the German school are to be found, did not appeal to the general taste. Other reasons are to be found in the character of German art, which has always tended toward subjectivity and exaltation, toward the particular rather than the general, the Baroque rather than the Classical. This is a point of artistic psychology, not of quality. Although even the best German art may have had few repercussions outside Germany, this does not mean that it was not great. Grünewald's painting had no influence, yet remains a supreme expression of the German mind in an age of spiritual turmoil.

German painting has always shown a tendency to remain apart from current European movements, just as Germany was often out of step with the rest of Europe in its view of the social position of the artist. Dürer never received the recognition and patronage enjoyed by Leonardo and Michelangelo, although his powers equaled theirs.

The beginning of German painting

German painting began in the 8th and 9th centuries with the first Christian missionaries who brought with them manuscripts from as far as Byzantium. They established scriptoria in which these venerated manuscripts served as models for the scribes. They also commissioned for their churches wall-paintings in which biblical stories and the concepts of Christianity were visually expounded. Of this early monumental painting almost nothing has survived.

There exists, however, a rich store of medieval manuscript illumination. The Ada Gospels (p. 47) suggest the first native flowering of the craft in Carolingian times.

The Reichenau manuscript, reproduced on p. 73, shows the dramatic expressiveness of the art of the Ottonian period (mid-10th to mid-11th centuries) centered in the monasteries of Reichenau Island in Lake Constance, while the 12th-century Cologne manuscript (p. 74) reveals a characteristic German Romanesque illumination of bold statuesque style. For the most part well preserved, these brightly illuminated pages are some compensation for the loss of wall-paintings.

The same laws of style applied to both large-scale painting and manuscript illumination well into the 15th century. The designs of both went back to the same "pattern books," and the miniatures were frequently painted by the same masters who worked on devotional panels and altarpieces. It is natural that small panel paintings should differ little from miniatures in color or style, but larger paintings also resembled the small forms. The painter of altarpieces did not work more elaborately because he had more space and a larger audience, nor was the miniature painter more delicate or cursory in his smaller format. Scale was not yet a determining factor of style.

The ill-defined frontiers of the German school

The compass of the German school is as hard to determine as is the "Germanness" of German art. Germany has seldom enjoyed precise geographical borders. It has been debated whether Veit Stoss should be called German rather than Polish, or whether Konrad Witz was Swiss rather than German. There are also the painters who were born and worked in what today constitutes Austria. The distinction between Netherlandish and German painting has always been more pronounced, but it must not be forgotten that until about 1600 the borders between these regions were not clearly defined.

Early altarpieces

The earliest types of panel painting were done for the Church, just as wall-painting and book illumination had been. The *Altarpiece from Soest* (p. 75) is an example of the retable, which was placed at the back of the altar. From the beginning of the 14th century, reliquaries in the form of huge cupboards filled with carved figures of sacred personages were often set up on altars to replace the traditional house-like reliquaries. Soon the shutters of the cupboards began to be painted, and the first altarpieces of the modern type developed. Sometimes on their backs or frames there were niches that contained relics, as in the Cologne triptych (p. 76).

Painting as a craft

Painters were organized in guilds and looked upon as craftsmen. They were put under solemn contracts that included directions about subject matter and provided advance payments to buy materials. They had to maintain workshops, with assistants and apprentices. As can be seen in the examples on pages 75, 76, and 77, the borders of early pictures were carved out of the same panels that served for the paintings. The custom continued into the 16th century, when artists amused their patrons by painting a sitter's gloves, perhaps, onto a frame, as though hanging out of the picture.

The establishment of local schools

The earliest paintings that can be grouped into distinct schools come from the oldest Christian centers in West Germany. Like the manuscripts, these paintings traveled surprisingly far at times, chiefly along the trade routes. Secular as well as spiritual centers provided meeting points for artists and their clients.

In the latter half of the 14th century the Holy Roman Emperor Charles IV took up residence in Prague. As the little local school was incapable of meeting the large demands made upon it, artists and works of art were imported from all over the Empire and from Italy. It will never be known who painted the exquisitely Italianate *Madonna and Child from Glatz* (p. 78), but it was a certain Master Theodorich who adorned the walls of the chapel at Karlstein Castle with strongly expressive panel paintings in a style derived from Giotto.

The down-to-earth Bohemian style is to be found at the same time at Hamburg. Master Bertram, who worked there, was a man of more than one skill, like so many medieval artists. His paintings grace a large altarpiece of the cupboard type, for which his workshop supplied the many statues of saints. The connection between Hamburg and Prague is explained by the cross-currents of influence within European art and the journeyman trips that the painters undertook. It is more remarkable that side by side with the stocky figures and matter-of-fact story-telling of Master Bertram's *God Creating the Animals* (p. 77) there existed the delicate, pretty style of Westphalia and the Rhineland (pp. 80, 81, and 82). These regions had closer links with France, and were stimulated by the refined and rather fragile style in vogue at the courts of Burgundy and Paris, although the German artists never reached the extremes of courtly fantasy found in France.

The Cologne School

When the court of Prague dissolved, the centers of art shifted back to West and South Germany. During the 15th century Cologne was among the foremost cities of Europe. Here the gracious style of the first half of the century culminated in the work of Stefan Lochner. The Cologne School is characterized by a lack of drama or psychological interest, and by pleasantly light colors. None of these features, however, is to be found in the work of its best representative, the Master of the St. Bartholomew Altarpiece, one of the most poignant dramatists and imaginative colorists of his age (p. 86).

Konrad Witz

The Paris School of the early part of the 15th century influenced other regions beside the Rhineland. For example, Master Francke extended its influence to Hamburg. In Basel the airy International Gothic style of the first third of the century was outdated by Konrad Witz. He produced massively sober panels, such as *Joachim and Anna at the Golden Gate* (p. 84), that describe the everyday world with a realism never before achieved, and different from that emerging in the southern Netherlands. While Jan van Eyck was essentially a painstaking miniaturist in his approach, Witz would leave a figure or a composition as soon as he had made its general lines apparent. Both were realist painters, but Witz's work has an impact that shows that in spirit he was akin to his Florentine contemporary Masaccio. In Florence the time was ripe for the Renaissance to begin, but in Basel a solitary genius shone and was forgotten.

Albrecht Dürer and the Italian Renaissance

The Italian Renaissance began to make an impression on German painting at the end of the 15th century. It is certain that the Tyrolese Michael Pacher knew the work of Mantegna, although he did not imitate his pagan, antique vocabulary, but only his forceful syntax of perspective, as shown in *St. Wolfgang Forces the Devil to Hold the Prayerbook for Him* (p. 85).

Nuremberg produced in Albrecht Dürer the first northern painter of both artistic and intellectual genius. Dürer possessed an inquiring mind of enormous energy. He introduced the curiosity, the control, and the analytical approach that characterize the Renaissance into a world that, unlike Italy, had not been prepared by decades of classical studies. His work must not be judged by the extent to which it visibly approached the Italian style. His style never entirely lost its Gothic qualities; indeed this characteristic endeared his engravings to some of the first Italian Mannerists even in his own lifetime. It was the spirit he once expressed in the phrase "art before custom," the conscious creative process by which he shaped the inventions of his boundless imagination, that distinguished him from his contemporaries.

The German Renaissance

The first third of the 16th century saw an extraordinarily rich outburst of pictorial genius across Germany. Four of the artists who achieved greatness—Grünewald, Altdorfer, Hans Baldung, and Lucas Cranach—each created an intense personal vision.

Mathis Gothardt, called Grünewald, was the contemporary of Dürer, but completely unlike him. Grünewald's *Crucifixion* (p. 91) is proof that the ecstatic Gothic spirit continued to live in the age of Raphael and Dürer. Grünewald was acquainted with Renaissance perspective and space but, unlike Dürer, he used Renaissance techniques simply to heighten the emotional impact of his imagery. The terrible figure of Christ in the *Crucifixion* is medieval in its evocation of the agony and the ugliness of tortured death.

Albrecht Altdorfer, who traveled in the Austrian Alps and along the Danube, was the first landscape painter in the modern sense, painting scenery for its own beauty and not as a background to religious or mythological scenes. When figures appear in his paintings they are rather the complement of his landscapes; in both there is a subjective distortion. Altdorfer was the foremost painter of the Danube School, a group of sensitive southern German painters who painted imaginary views and atmospheric effects.

Hans Baldung, called Grien, was led by the ferment of the times to a vision as disturbing as that of Grünewald; however, his inspiration was not always religious, as can be seen in *Two Witches* (p. 93). New subjects from a nether world were breaking into German art, as they had in the work of the Flemish painter Hieronymus Bosch. Baldung was the paragon of the northern Mannerism that was the consequence, not of a brief Renaissance equipoise (as in Italy), but of an undecided struggle between old and new concepts.

Lucas Cranach passed from religious painting in the earlier, unreflective tradition to the piquancy of a courtly style. In 1505 he went to Wittenberg, where he became the friend of Martin Luther. In his early works, the importance of the landscape element links him with the Danube School. But in Wittenberg both his style and his commissions changed. All his life, Cranach continued to paint superb portraits. At the same time, in his mythological paintings, he developed a new type of female nude.

Hans Holbein the Younger

Hans Holbein grew up in Augsburg, the first German town to receive the influence of the southern Renaissance. Holbein probably visited Italy, and in Augsburg itself the Fugger family built and furnished its private chapel in an Italianate style as early as 1509. During Holbein's years on the Continent he produced mostly religious paintings. In England, the lack of religious commissions restricted him to portraiture. He gave his sitters an aloof air similar to that favored by eminent patrons in Italy and France, but he was almost alone in achieving a piercing directness of expression.

A lapse in artistic achievement

A period of indifferent work toward the middle of the 16th century was the result of continuous religious and political strife. The Reformation caused a dearth of religious commissions, while aesthetic ideals floundered in a general taste for the Italian style. There was no German painter forceful enough to find a common idiom for the many minor talents, while there were artists in the Netherlands and Italy who gained a wide following. Only portraits were distinguished by the traditional solid craftsmanship and gift of characterization. It became customary to spend prolonged periods of study, travel, and independent work in Italy, and by the end of the century there were painters who mastered the foreign idiom so completely that it is often hard to distinguish their work from that of their Italian contemporaries. An example of this is Hans von Aachen's *The Victory of Truth* (p. 96).

Landscape, still-life, and genre painting

On the other hand, landscape painting remained the exclusive domain of northerners, who were esteemed as specialists in this field even in Italy. Adam Elsheimer from Frankfurt outdid all the Flemings of his day with the variety of atmospheric phenomena and the range of light, color, and sentiment at his command (p. 98).

It was in the Netherlands, about 1600, that still-life began to be developed as a specialized branch of painting. In this field a German painter, Georg Flegel, also held his own, while Johann Liss represented large-scale genre painting (p. 99). These beginnings of German Baroque painting, as others of equal promise in sculpture and architecture, were cut short by the Thirty Years' War. Painters of portraits, such as Sandrart (p. 100), always looked to the Flemish and French schools as models, and it is only the self-possessed charm of expression that sets an occasional canvas apart.

The Baroque and the burghers

Painting began to flourish again at the turn of the 17th century as the patchwork of sovereignties that made up the Holy Roman Empire regained its stability, and patrons their affluence. The Catholic south forever demanded new altarpieces, and commissioned decorations and portraits in the grand manner. The Baroque paintings in this volume (pp. 101, 102, and 103) were chosen from among dozens of equally important examples.

Throughout the 18th century the level of accomplishment remained steady. In South Germany and Austria local schools became established. A more sober portraiture prevailed in the Protestant courts and among the middle classes of the north and east. These areas were pervaded in the last two decades of the 18th century by the tenets of Classicism, forming a counterpoint to southern exuberance, as in Tischbein's *Portrait of Goethe in the Campagna* (p. 104).

The end of tradition

The turn of the 18th century marked the end of a tradition of taste in painting that went back 300 years. After the French Revolution there were drastic changes throughout Europe. The role of the Catholic Church, traditionally a generous patron, was greatly altered. There was almost no demand for religious painting, and in architecture taste had reacted against the Baroque in favor of the chaste monochrome of Classicism. There were "Romantick" attempts, by men such as Schnorr von Carolsfeld (p. 108), to revive religious painting in a manner that was a compromise between the styles of medieval Germany, 15th-century Italy, and Classicism. But the most important achievements of German art in the 19th century were landscapes and portraits. Such pictures graced the houses of the growing middle class—thoughtful, self-assured, well-read citizens on whom literary allusions, or even the symbolism of a landscape, were rarely lost. Contrary to earlier fashions, genre painting was seldom merely entertaining, but didactic and at times of a genuinely religious nature, as in Wilhelm Leibl's *Three Women in Church* (p. 112). Even history painting attained occasional excellence in the classicist tradition, and there were many attempts to paint truly original themes such as "light," as in Adolf von Menzel's *Room with the Balcony* (p. 110), and "industry," as in Karl Blechen's *Ironworks at Eberswalde* (p. 109).

Von Menzel's work was popular in France, but it was not until the contents of his studio were exhibited after his death that the extent to which he had pioneered Impressionism in Germany was realized.

Biographies

SOME BOOKS FOR FURTHER READING

S. Sitwell, *German Baroque Art*, London, 1927.
H. Picton, *Early German Art and Its Origins*, London, 1939.
P. Bescargues, *German Painting from the 14th to the 16th Century*, London, 1958.

SEE ALSO UNDER THE INDIVIDUAL BIOGRAPHIES

HANS VON AACHEN

1552-1615

A Mannerist painter at the courts of Munich and Prague

Hans von Aachen was born in Cologne in 1552. His parents had had to leave their home town, Aachen, when it became dangerous for them to practice their religion there. Hans von Aachen's training with a Flemish painter in Cologne brought him into contact with Mannerism. In 1574 he went to Italy, remaining abroad for fourteen years. He spent most of this period in Venice, where he was deeply impressed by Tintoretto, then at the height of his powers. Master Hans had some success of his own as a painter of portraits and religious subjects. When he visited Florence, his sitters included the sculptor Giovanni da Bologna, the Grand Duke of Tuscany, and the poetess Donna Laura Terracina.

Back in Cologne in 1588, he worked on an altarpiece for the Church of St. Maria im Capitol. After a few months he left for the court of Duke William V of Bavaria at Munich. While in Bavaria he painted a large *Crucifixion* for the Munich Church of St. Michael and a *Coronation of the Virgin*, 1596, for St. Ulrich at Augsburg.

Meanwhile, his portrait of Giovanni da Bologna had come to the attention of the Holy Roman Emperor, Rudolph II, who thought it so outstanding that he made Master Hans a court painter and, in 1594, a noble, and allowed him a salary of 200 florins a year. On his marriage in Munich in 1596, Master Hans's wedding gift from the emperor was a silver-gilt drinking set. In 1601, yielding to these inducements, he settled in Prague.

Henceforth he made a speciality of mythological scenes containing preciously posed female nudes, for the pleasure of Rudolph II. Despite their erotic undertones, these small paintings have a sophistication that ranks them among the finest productions of Northern Mannerism. It was also the duty of Master Hans to paint portraits of the foreign princesses who were possible brides for his patron. One such mission took him back to Italy in 1603. In 1615 he died in Prague.

Ecce Homo (detail) 1600
London, Courtauld Inst. Gall.

ACH.

HIS WORKS INCLUDE

The Victory of Truth, 1598
Munich, Alte Pin.

Mythological Scenes
Vienna, Kunsthist. Mus.

See also page 96

ALBRECHT ALTDORFER

about 1480-1538

The first European painter of landscape in the modern sense

Albrecht Altdorfer was born about 1480, probably at Regensburg on the Danube, the son of a painter. He studied at Amberg and returned to his home town some time before 1505. There he prospered, as painter, architect to the city and a town councilor. When the Jews were expelled from Regensburg and their synagogue destroyed, he supervised the building of a pilgrimage chapel of the Beautiful Mary on its site. This was consecrated in 1519. It is possible that Altdorfer's panel of *The Madonna and Child*, painted in the Byzantine manner, is the picture of the *Beautiful Mary* that was once venerated in this chapel as the miraculous icon of the Madonna painted by St. Luke.

Altdorfer's will of 1528 and an inventory of his possessions still survive to testify

St. George in the Forest (detail) 1510
Munich, Alte Pin.

Landscape with a Footbridge
London, N. G.

to his prosperity. He died in Regensburg in 1538, the leading master of the Danube School.

Like his older contemporaries Grünewald and Dürer, Altdorfer was aware of the intellectual currents that were sweeping over medieval Germany and introducing a new era. This awareness, together with his own romantic conception and his outstanding sense of color, depth, and light, made him an innovator of genius. He had no successor until Adam Elsheimer nearly 100 years later.

Altdorfer's earliest paintings, among them a few small panels dated 1507, suggest that he knew something of book illumination. He was certainly influenced by Dürer and Michael Pacher, and by the early landscape settings of Lucas Cranach the Elder. In 1511 Altdorfer made a journey down the Danube into upper and lower Austria, and the Alpine scenery gave a lasting romanticism to his landscape style. As early as 1510, however, the little panel *St. George in the Forest* had revealed his extraordinary ability as a landscape painter. The tiny figure of St. George on horseback is almost lost among the luxuriant forest trees.

Until about 1515 the characteristics of Altdorfer's work were light colors, a sketchy style, and a tendency toward elongated, mannered figures. The figures

The Battle of Arbela (detail) 1529
Munich, Alte Pin.

The Battle of Arbela (detail) 1529
Munich, Alte Pin.

remained expressively distorted during his middle period, but the color became richer and more visionary. He accepted larger commissions, such as the altarpiece for the Church of the Minorites in Regensburg, 1517.

One of the best-known works of Altdorfer's late period is the small panel *The Battle of Arbela*, 1529, of which the upper half shows a grandiose evening sky above an exquisitely rendered seascape, and the lower half a vast, densely packed battle scene treated with miniature-like precision. In many of his religious paintings, too—*The Nativity*, for example, or *Susanna at the Bath*—the figures are reduced almost to insignificance. Often they are difficult to find among the background ruins.

Many designs for woodcuts and engravings survive, including some, in a style adapted to Dürer's, that were done for the Holy Roman Emperor Maximilian I. But practically nothing remains of Altdorfer's architectural work. His importance in this field can only be deduced from the magnificent buildings in his drawings and paintings, although the drawings, often landscapes in delicate *chiaroscuro*, were intended not as studies but as works of art in their own right.

E. Waldmann Albrecht Altdorfer London, 1923

EGID QUIRIN ASAM   1692-1750

A versatile master of the decorative possibilities of sculpture, architecture, and painting

Egid Quirin Asam was born at Tegernsee, Bavaria, in 1692, into a family of painters, of which his father, Hans Georg Asam, was the most distinguished. Egid Quirin and his elder brother and lifelong collaborator, Cosmas Damian Asam, were trained as painters in their father's workshop until they went to Rome together in 1712. During the two years they spent there Egid Quirin studied sculpture at the Academy of St. Luke, breathing the atmosphere of the Roman Baroque in general and the school of Bernini in particular. These stimulants remained with him all his life, giving a foundation of solidity to the pathos and ecstasy of his own inspiration.

Both brothers were also architects and at their best when, as in one of their first joint enterprises, the monastery church at Weltenburg in Bavaria, 1716-21, they were together responsible for the architecture and interior decoration. Egid Quirin managed the sculpture and plasterwork, and Cosmas Damian the painting. They were the first to unify all the different surfaces of a building. Architecture merged imperceptibly into painted stucco, stucco into illusionistic painting, the whole designed to draw the eye irresistibly upward to the religious visions covering the dome.

Egid Quirin's outstanding achievement at Weltenburg was the statue of St. George upon the high altar, a figure saturated with late Baroque theatricality. The golden-haired saint on his prancing horse was placed with the light falling on him from behind so that he appears to be riding into the church.

Design for a Round Chapel
(detail) 1730
Munich, Staatl. Graphische Samm.

The brothers' fame was now secure. Commissions poured into their studio in Munich. Important ecclesiastical projects were fulfilled in rapid succession in the light Rococo style then becoming fashionable throughout southern Germany. The last and best-known product of the brothers' collaboration was a church dedicated to St. John Nepomuk that they built and lavishly adorned at their own expense on a piece of land adjoining one of Egid Quirin's Munich houses.

Cosmas Damian died in 1739. Egid Quirin outlived him by 11 years, during which time he saw to the frescoes as well as the sculpture and stucco work of his decorative schemes. He died in 1750, while working at Mannheim.

St. Dorothy (detail) about 1410-25
Munich, Staatl. Graphische Samm.

See also page 113

BAVARIA, ST. DOROTHY   about 1410-25

Bavarian woodcut

Toward the end of the 14th century, block printing first appeared and became popular in Germany. The process was simple. The design was transferred to a block of wood. The parts not to be printed were cut away and the design, now in relief, was heavily inked over and transferred to paper by means of a press. The resulting prints were usually hand colored in strong hues to make them resemble the more expensive miniatures.

The simple technique of block printing was the basis upon which all later developments in printing and engraving have been built. Northern Italy, the Netherlands, France, and Germany have each been thought to be its country of origin. Germany's claim is substantiated by the large number of early prints surviving there. They were in enormous demand in Germany from the beginning of the 15th century, owing to their relative cheapness. The block was comparatively easy to make and each block could produce a few hundred prints, which were inexpensive and therefore accessible to the less wealthy members of society in a way that the less ephemeral art treasures had never been. The subjects were mostly religious and moral, issued at first in single sheets and, from the middle of the 15th century on, in series and as book illustrations.

This large-scale production did not play any part in the great pictorial innovations, the new realism, and the representation of space, to be found in the painting and sculpture of the time. Stylistically, the early woodcuts were closely linked with an older Gothic tradition. The print *St. Dorothy* provides a good example of the two-dimensional style in which the first colored woodcuts were executed. It came from the monastery of St. Zeno near Reichenhall, Bavaria, where it was later attached to the cover of a manuscript which had been written in 1410. St. Dorothy, a large figure in an elaborately draped cloak, bends to grasp the hand of the tiny Christ Child. According to legend she presented the Child with a basket of fruit, which He carries here. The background is filled out with a formal spray of roses that takes an integral part in the flat design.

20

KARL BLECHEN

A pioneer of realistic landscape painting

Karl Blechen was born in 1798 at Kottbus in eastern Germany, the son of a revenue official of limited means. As soon as he left school Blechen took a post in a bank. He devoted all his free time to art, making such progress that at 24 he entered the Berlin Academy. There he spent a year studying landscape painting.

A journey to Dresden in 1823 brought him into contact with the Romantic landscapists Friedrich and his friend J.C.C. Dahl. Later the architect Karl Schinkel took an interest in his work and provided him with a job painting scenery for the newly built Königstädtisches Theater in Berlin, where Blechen also found time to produce many romantic theatrical landscapes. *Mountain Gorge in Winter*, one of the best, owes as much to Friedrich as to his own dramatic vision. In 1828 he showed his large *Camp of the Semnones*. In this the classical warriors are but incidental to the landscape, which was the real subject of Blechen's interest.

In 1827 he had resigned from the theater and the next year he spent some time in Rome, then went on to Naples and beyond. The Italian scenery had as deep an effect on him as it had had on Camille Corot shortly before. It curbed Blechen's romanticism and led him to a more objective, observant view of nature and a natural treatment of light. He made many sketches that he worked up on his return to Germany, after more than a year abroad, into large paintings. The resulting realistic landscapes had little popular appeal, but a small circle of friends and patrons shielded Blechen from financial failure.

In the last years of his life his output consisted of studies of Berlin gardens and backyards and other simple themes, in which he used a restriction of detail and an austerity of composition to great expressive effect. About 1834 he painted one of the first industrial landscapes, *The Ironworks at Eberswalde*.

Blechen's career ended tragically with the loss of his reason in 1839. He died in Berlin the following year, at the age of 42.

Self-portrait, 1822
West Berlin, Staatl. Mus.

HIS WORKS INCLUDE

The Ironworks at Eberswalde
about 1834
West Berlin, Staatl. Mus.
Sanssouci Palace, about 1835
West Berlin, Staatl. Mus.

See also page 109

Palmhouse (detail) about 1832
West Berlin, Staatl. Mus.

The Avio Falls at Tivoli, about 1830
West Berlin, Staatl. Mus.

The Madonna and Child from Glatz
(detail) about 1350
West Berlin, Staatl. Mus.

See also page 78

BOHEMIA, THE MADONNA AND CHILD FROM GLATZ
about 1350

A painted panel of Gothic grace

The evolution of Bohemian painting began a little before the middle of the 14th century under Charles I of Bohemia, who later became Holy Roman Emperor, Charles IV. Brought up and educated in Paris, energetic and cultured, Charles made Prague his favorite residence and encouraged leading scholars and artists to come and work there. As he had interests and connections as far way as Avignon, then the seat of the popes, and northern Italy, the Bohemian school acquired an international character.

The school divides into three phases. The first, still linked with German painting of the earlier 14th century, is characterized by the Hohenfurth (Czech: Vyssi Brod) panels of *The Life and Passion of Christ*. From the same workshop, perhaps even a later production of the same hand, came the painted panel of *The Madonna and Child* that presumably once belonged to a Franciscan monastery at Glatz in Bohemia. The presence of the donor, Ernst of Pardubic, first archbishop of Prague, a tiny figure at the extreme left, dates the panel between 1344 and 1364, probably about 1350. The Madonna, seated on a realistic throne, has a solidity that was new at the time, though something of Gothic remoteness lingers in her expression.

The revolutionary features that were thus only beginning to emerge in the first phase of the Bohemian school reached maturity in the second, with the massive realism of 127 portraits of saints and prophets painted by Master Theodoric for the chapel of Karlstein Castle near Prague. The third Bohemian style of repute was dominated by the Master of Wittingau (Czech: Trebon), active about 1380.

The Madonna and Child from
Krumau (detail) about 1400
Vienna, Kunsthist. Mus.

See also page 134

BOHEMIA?, THE MADONNA AND CHILD FROM KRUMAU
about 1400

A Late Gothic stone Madonna by an unknown sculptor

A stone figure of *The Madonna and Child*, nearly four feet high, is known by the name of the monastery of Krumau (Czech: Cesky Krumlov) in southern Bohemia, to which it formerly belonged. Only traces of the original polychrome painting remain, but the subtle modeling and the play of light and shade among the deep, elegant folds of drapery alone make the figure of one of the finest examples of the International Gothic style. Other distinguishing virtues are the tender characterization of the face and a pervasive lyricism.

The statue is one of a series of sculptured madonnas found in many parts of eastern Europe, Silesia, Bohemia, Austria, and Germany, known collectively as the Beautiful Madonnas. It is possible that the type was invented by a single itinerant artist of genius. If so, he may have come originally from either Salzburg or the Rhineland to work mostly in northern Germany, Silesia, Poland, and Bohemia; or he may have started out from Bohemia.

HANS BURGKMAIR

A painter and woodcut designer of Augsburg

Esther before Ahasuerus (detail) 1528
Munich, Alte Pin.

Hans Burgkmair was born in Augsburg in 1473, almost the exact contemporary of Dürer. He was trained by his father, the painter Thomas Burgkmair, and then at Colmar in Alsace by Martin Schongauer. He traveled as a journeyman painter to the upper Rhine and, when he was 21, to Italy, a visit that coincided with Dürer's Italian visit of 1494 to 1495. About 1506 Burgkmair went to Italy for the second time and stayed in Venice, when Dürer happened again to be in that city at the same time.

Burgkmair had joined the Augsburg painters' guild in 1498, though his dated works do not begin until 1501. The ease with which he could adapt his knowledge of Italian painting and introduce Italian Renaissance architecture into such pictures as *The Basilicas*, 1504, assured him early success in his home town. But in, for example, his *Coronation of the Virgin*, 1507, although the Late Gothic characteristics that still remain are blended with luxuriant Renaissance decoration, the composition is timid, with none of the feeling for depth and volume that marks Dürer's work of the same period.

As a designer of woodcuts Burgkmair was in great demand, especially at the court of the Holy Roman Emperor Maximilian I. For five years, from 1512, he seems to have worked exclusively in this medium. He collaborated with Dürer and other artists on drawings for the emperor's large woodcuts *The Triumphal Arch* and *The Triumphal Procession*, and on illustrations for a great number of books commissioned by the emperor.

From 1518 until his death in Augsburg in October, 1531, Burgkmair worked once more chiefly as a painter, revealing a gifted and progressive talent. His color, in the Venetian manner, became more intense, his landscape more dramatic, and his handling of human figures less restricted. In his attempts to express emotion, however, Burgkmair never achieved more than a rather empty pathos.

HIS WORKS INCLUDE

The Basilicas, 1504
Augsburg, Gal.

The Madonna and Child, 1509
Nuremberg, Germanisches Nationalmus.

Altarpiece of St. John, 1518
Munich, Alte Pin.

Esther before Ahasuerus, 1528
Munich, Alte Pin.

See also pages 90, 122

ASMUS JAKOB CARSTENS

A passionate classicist

Atropos (detail) 1794
Frankfurt-am-Main, Städelsches Kunstinst.

Asmus Jakob Carstens was born in 1754 in St. Jürgen, Schleswig-Holstein, the son of a miller. Orphaned as a very young child, he was brought up by guardians who refused to allow him to take up painting and apprenticed him instead to a cooper at Eckernförde. However, he taught himself drawing and art theory. Leaving his job as soon as he came of age in 1775, he went to Copenhagen.

At first Carstens' rebellious nature and scorn of tradition prevented him from entering the Copenhagen Academy. He preferred to work on his own, making a careful study, but no copies, of the old masters. Eventually he decided that he must go to Italy in order to paint classical and historical themes.

He therefore joined the academy in the hope of finding material support for his

Self-portrait (detail)
Hamburg, Kunsthalle

HIS WORKS INCLUDE

Ganymede, about 1795
Weimar, Schlossmus.

Jason
Weimar, Schlossmus.

See also page 126

See also page 76

plans. But in 1783, as he consistently ignored the advice offered him and finally refused a medal that he won, he was expelled. He started at once on the journey to Italy with his own meager savings, taking with him his younger brother Frederik, also a painter. Before they returned to Germany, Carstens saw Leonardo's *Last Supper* in Milan and Giulio Romano's frescoes at the Palazzo del Tè in Mantua. It soon became his ambition to paint frescoes on a large scale.

At Lübeck for a few years, he scraped a living by painting portraits, while he carried on with the larger compositions and studies that were nearer his heart. In 1787 patrons and friends financed a move to Berlin. There, the same year, Carstens' large drawing *The Fall of the Rebel Angels* won admiration and brought him a fresco commission from the minister von Heinitz, in whose Berlin house he painted his *Apollo and the Muses*, destroyed in 1867. The only other fresco that he ever painted was a grisaille ceiling (also lost) for the bedroom of the queen of Prussia. He owed this commission to the good offices of the architect Giovanni Genelli, with whom he collaborated on a monument to Frederick the Great of Prussia. Their model for this was destroyed in 1806, so that all that is left of Carstens' sculpture is the plaster cast of a figure of Atropos.

After three years in Berlin, Carstens was appointed a professor at the academy and two years later he was granted leave of absence to travel to Italy. Once in Rome, he stayed for the remaining six years of his life. He refused to return to the Berlin Academy, but delivered a diatribe on the tyranny and materialism prevalent there. He was dismissed *in absentia*. This antipathy to compromise made him one of the most isolated artists of his day.

In Rome he was able to study in detail the works of Michelangelo. Carstens' classicism, unlike that of most of his contemporaries, was inherent rather than superimposed, natural rather than acquired. The numerous drawings of his last years in Rome, whether illustrations of classical mythology or inventions of his own, were inspired by a deep understanding of classic form and achieved an appropriately expressive rhythm of line.

Carstens produced very few oil paintings, perhaps because his interest in color was half-hearted at best. Nor was even one of the large cartoons and drawings of his Rome period ever actually translated into fresco. Yet throughout these years he continued to work like one possessed. Although his health was failing, he was as incapable of sparing himself as of compromising with others. He contracted tuberculosis, and died in 1798.

COLOGNE, THE CRUCIFIXION   about 1320

A Crucifixion triptych of the narrative type

At the beginning of the 14th century Cologne was one of the most important centers of Gothic painting in Germany. Fresco fragments in the Church of St. Cecilia, paintings on the cathedral choir screen, and a number of illuminated manuscripts still bear witness to the fact. Among the latter, two separate trends may be distinguished from the beginning: a lively narrative idiom of lyrical charm, and a heavier, more popular style.

Gothic panel paintings, similarly of two kinds, also survive from this early phase of the Cologne School. Of these, the well-preserved *Crucifixion* triptych of about 1320 is one of the finest examples of the narrative type. The painter has given an almost metallic precision to the folds of the draperies, so that their elegant linear rhythm effectively emphasizes the flat, two-dimensional character of the composition. The events are related in a melancholy manner. The ornamented gold background lifts the figures into an unreal, heavenly space.

The frame surrounding the panels contains small rectangular niches that once held relics.

The Crucifixion (detail) about 1320
Cologne, Wallraf-Richartz-Mus.

LUCAS CRANACH the ELDER 1472-1553

A courtly painter of new Italian forms in a traditional Gothic framework

Lucas Cranach was born in 1472 at Kronach (hence the name by which he was known) in Franconia. He stayed in Kronach until at least 1498 while his father, a painter, taught him his craft.

There are no known works by Cranach before about 1500. In that year, already nearly 30 years old, he went to Vienna. On his way there he must have visited Nuremberg, where Dürer was working, and the towns of the Danube valley. Certainly the small panel paintings and woodcuts that he produced in Vienna, between 1500 and 1504, reveal him up-to-date with new developments in Germany. Yet even then he had an independent vision, and in landscape in particular he was a pioneer. The charming landscape settings of works like *The Crucifixion*, about 1500, antedate any known landscapes of the Danube School. In fact, they made a profound impression on the chief master of the school, Albrecht Altdorfer, when he stopped in Vienna during his trip to Austria.

Self-portrait
Florence, Uffizi

Cranach moved in the most intellectual circles of Viennese society. Four of his portraits were of university men and their wives. He himself married a woman of patrician birth, Barbara Brengbier.

In 1504, after four years in Vienna, Cranach was sufficiently known to be offered the position of court painter to the elector of Saxony, Frederick the Wise. The elector was bent on turning the town of Wittenberg, where he had established his court, from a cultural backwater into a center of learning and the arts. He founded a university to which he invited scholars from every part of Germany. In this young, thriving society Cranach settled in 1505, to embark on a career as an artist that was equaled only by his career as citizen, councilor, and mayor of Wittenberg. In 1508 he was sent, probably on a diplomatic mission, to the Netherlands. In Antwerp he made a portrait of the future Holy Roman Emperor Charles V, then a boy of eight. He was raised to the nobility and granted a coat of arms consisting of a winged serpent.

At the same time, Martin Luther was appointed professor of theology in 1508 at

Konrad Krebs, about 1540
Reims, France, Mus.

Adam and Eve, 1535
West Berlin, Staatl. Mus.

Wittenberg. With the Reformation the town became a hub of Protestantism. Cranach met the champions of the reformed faith, whose characters he illumined in numerous able portraits. Several of them, including Luther himself, godfather to one of Cranach's children and the subject of many portraits, became his friends.

Cranach's Wittenberg studio rapidly acquired a prodigious reputation. Soon it was working at full capacity on paintings, etchings, and woodcuts, which it issued with the mark of the winged serpent. There were large altarpieces destined for Protestant churches; woodcut illustrations for Luther's Bible and for the writings of other Protestant scholars; and religious works ordered by Catholic patrons, such as Cardinal Albrecht of Brandenburg, whom Cranach painted in prayer before a crucifix and as St. Jerome. There were also portraits, and mythological pictures that served as a setting for the female nude. This nude was converted by Cranach from an Italian Mannerist model into a peculiarly characteristic type of his own.

As court painter Cranach had to supervise palaces in the process of decoration, design stained-glass windows for them and illustrate books for their libraries. He ran an apothecary's shop, and a publishing house that created a wide market for works of Protestant scholarship. His two sons, Hans and Lucas the Younger, both became painters and it is often difficult to distinguish their work from the father's.

Duke Moritz of Saxony
Reims, France, Mus.

The Judgment of Paris (detail) 1527
Copenhagen, Statens Mus.

Hans died on a visit to Italy in 1537. Lucas eventually managed the workshop, carrying on the Cranach tradition until his death in 1586.

Meanwhile, after the death of Frederick the Wise in 1532, the elder Cranach remained in the service of the succeeding electors John the Steadfast and, finally, John Frederick the Magnanimous. The latter joined forces with other Lutheran princes against the Holy Roman Emperor Charles V and was taken prisoner at Mühlberg. During the subsequent siege of Wittenberg in 1544, Cranach was summoned to a friendly audience with the emperor, who wished to know whether it was he or the younger Lucas who had painted a certain picture in his possession. Evidently it was difficult even then to decide the authorship of products of the Cranach workshop. The painter was able to plead for mercy for his patron, who was eventually banished to Augsburg. At his repeated request Cranach, by then an old man, left Wittenberg to join him there. When the elector was pardoned a few years later and made a prince of the empire, both took up residence in Weimar. There Cranach lived, in the house of a married daughter, until his death on October 16, 1553, at the age of 81.

E. Ruhmer Cranach London, 1963

HIS WORKS INCLUDE

The Crucifixion, about 1500
Vienna, Kunsthist. Mus.

Portrait of Dr. Johann Stefan Reuss
and his Wife, 1503
Nuremberg, Germanisches Nationalmus.

Portrait of John Frederick
the Magnanimous, 1531
Paris, Louvre

Adam and Eve, 1535
West Berlin, Staatl. Mus.

See also page 87

GEORG RAPHAEL DONNER   1693-1741

A sculptor who brought a new, classical restraint to the Baroque

Georg Raphael Donner was born at Esslingen in southern Germany in 1693. He studied sculpture in Austria, first in Vienna, then at the monastery of Heiligenkreuz outside the city under an Italian, Giovanni Giuliani. He visited Italy himself at the age of 22. Four years later he was living in Vienna with a wife and son.

In 1729 Donner revisited Italy to purchase marble, presumably on behalf of Count Esterházy, whose court sculptor he afterwards became. This post took him to live in Pressburg (now Bratislava), where he had a large workshop and many pupils. For the Elymosynarius Chapel there, he made a kneeling figure in white marble and reliefs of the Passion in lead, a material to which he later frequently reverted because of its smooth surface. His high altar at Bratislava Cathedral, 1733-35, (now dismantled) was partly of lead.

When Donner returned in 1734 to Vienna, where he spent the last seven years of his life, his style was mature. The turbulent heaviness characteristic of the contemporary Baroque sculpture was kept under control in his work by slow, dignified rhythms. At the same time, his sensitivity to human beauty maintained the emphasis on fullness of form. In his marble *Apotheosis of Emperor Charles VI*, 1734, he deliberately offset the powerful Roman-type figure of the emperor with the cool, classical beauty of the Winged Victory who crowns him.

The Apotheosis of
Emperor Charles VI, 1734
Vienna, Österreichische Gal.

HIS WORKS INCLUDE

The Passion of Christ, 1732
*Bratislava, Czechoslovakia,
Elymosynarius Chapel*

Perseus and Andromeda
Fountain, 1741
Vienna, Old Town Hall

See also page 143

Self-portrait, 1493
Paris, Louvre

The first Northern artist to grasp the spirit of the Italian Renaissance

Albrecht Dürer was a painter, graphic artist, and humanist of immense intellectual capacity. He was interested in mathematics, geography, and architecture, wrote treatises on geometry and perspective, 1525, fortification, 1527, and proportion, and left a great deal of manuscript material for a treatise on the theory of art. Thus he was the first artist north of the Alps to work in the spirit of the Italian Renaissance. He knew the leading European artists of his day, exchanging drawings with Raphael and painting portraits of Netherlandish artists such as Bernaert van Orley and Lucas van Leyden. In Germany his friends were humanist scholars belonging to a stratum of society well above that in which contemporary artists usually mixed. His closest friend was Willibald Pirkheimer, who had studied at Padua. He sympathized with Martin Luther and knew other leaders of the Reformation.

Dürer's father had come from Hungary to settle in Nuremberg, where he worked as a goldsmith. Albrecht, his second and favorite son, was born in 1471 and

Oswolt Krel, 1499
Munich, Alte Pin.

apprenticed as goldsmith to him at the age of 11. However, the young Dürer had a precocious talent for drawing (an example is a silverpoint self-portrait done when he was 13) and an overriding desire to become a painter. In 1488 he was allowed to enter the workshop of the Nuremberg painter and woodcut designer Michael Wolgemut, one of the busiest in Germany.

When he was 19 Dürer set out as a journeyman for Colmar, intending to seek out Martin Schongauer. But by the time he reached Colmar late in 1491, the master was already dead. Dürer moved on to Basel, where he did some woodcut designs, and then to Strasbourg. In 1494 he returned to Nuremberg and married. From the autumn of that year until the following spring he was in Italy for the first time, probably in Padua and Venice. It was ten years before he went to Italy again. Well known by then, he stayed for two years, 1505-7, mostly in Venice. Back in Nuremberg from 1507 to 1512, he devoted much of his time to painting.

In 1512, the Holy Roman Emperor Maximilian I appointed Dürer his court painter, employing him with other artists on designs for huge woodcuts of a

St. Jerome in his Cell (detail) 1514
(woodcut)
London, B. M., et al.

The Promenade, about 1496 (engraving)
London, B. M., et al.

The Knight, Death, and the Devil, 1513, (engraving)
London, B. M., et al.

29

Adam: from Adam and Eve, 1507
Madrid, Prado

triumphal arch and triumphal procession. Maximilian died in 1519. In 1520 Dürer started for the Netherlands with his wife to get his title and pension as court painter confirmed by the new emperor, Charles V, at Mechelen. This journey, recorded from day to day in Dürer's diary and sketches, was in the nature of a personal triumph. He visited many cities—Ghent, Bruges, Brussels—and met leading painters and men of letters, including Erasmus of Rotterdam. But a visit to Zeeland, where he went into the marshes to sketch a dead whale that had been washed ashore, gave him a high fever. He never recovered his health, though he continued to work with undiminished ardor until his death at Nuremberg in 1528.

The impact of Italian Renaissance art upon Dürer after his first visit to Italy was not immediately apparent, for he turned first to copper engraving and woodcuts. One of his most celebrated works is the woodcut series *The Apocalypse*, finished in 1498. The spirit of this as of two other sets, *The Small Passion* and *The Life of the Virgin*, is not that of the new Renaissance but of the old Late Gothic. In them Dürer seems primarily to have understood the potentialities of Schongauer's art, and to have created a heroic finale to the German medieval tradition.

In the single engravings and woodcuts, however, his intention to rival the Italians—Bellini, Mantegna, the Pollaiuoli—on their own ground is much clearer. In particular, he was stimulated by their skill in depicting the nude. Early plates such as *The Men's Bathhouse*, *St. Sebastian*, and *Jealousy* show the way in which he struggled with these unfamiliar forms. The highlight among these attempts is the engraving *Adam and Eve* of 1504.

During the years 1512 to 1520, which Dürer spent mainly engraving, he produced his three best plates, *The Knight, Death, and the Devil*, 1513, *St. Jerome in his Cell*, 1514, and *Melencolia*, 1514, as well as engravings of *The Virgin and Child* and the woodcut designs for Emperor Maximilian.

As a painter Dürer was never so prolific. The early period, before 1507, is best illustrated by a series of portraits beginning early in the 1490's and by one or two religious paintings. Two of the best known self-portraits, of 1498 and 1500, display the new self-assurance of the age of humanism. But it was only after 1507 and Dürer's second return from Italy that the full measure of his absorption of Renaissance art became clear, in paintings like the *Adam and Eve* of 1507 or *The Adoration of the Holy Trinity* of 1511.

To Dürer's last period, after 1520, belong some of his best portraits. In 1521 on his return from abroad he seems, despite increasing ill health, to have projected a number of religious paintings. For most of them, however, only the drawings were carried out. His last painting, the monumental *Four Apostles* of 1526, was an uncommissioned work that he presented to his native city, Nuremberg. Bellini's influence reappears here and adds a majestic dignity to Dürer's own fiery spirit.

Many drawings survive, including studies of hands, draperies and costume, portraits, and intimate drawings of the Virgin and Child. There are also many exquisite watercolors of flowers, animals, and landscape.

W. Waetzoldt Dürer and his Time London, 1950
E. Panofsky Albrecht Dürer (2 vols.) Princeton, 1953

ADAM ELSHEIMER

A landscape painter who explored the effects of light

Adam Elsheimer was born in 1578 in Frankfurt-am-Main, where he received his first art lessons under a local painter, Philipp Uffenbach. He seems also to have been influenced by the Flemish immigrant landscape painters living in nearby Frankenthal. At 20 Elsheimer went to Venice. Two years later, in 1600, he settled in Rome, where he remained until his death at the age of 32.

In Venice he was a pupil of his compatriot Johann Rottenhammer, a painter of easy charm whose work made little impression on him. It was much more the impact of the Venetians themselves that shaped his early style.

Elsheimer soon found that the visionary quality of his compositions could be enhanced by the clever use of light. Later, in his Rome period, he gave an almost impenetrable effect to the shadowy parts of a picture by placing different kinds of light—for example, moonlight or flickering firelight—at various points in it. *The Flight into Egypt*, 1609, provides a good example of this. Annibale Carracci and the master of *chiaroscuro*, Caravaggio, were working in Rome at the time, and Elsheimer admired both. But his art was always more intimate than theirs, and his interpretation of landscape a new one. His meticulously rendered settings were as important to him as the little figure groups that he blended into them.

His paintings, generally on copper and small, were successful. Rubens, who was a personal friend, considered his premature death a disaster for painting. Paul Bril was also a friend of Elsheimer. His significance, in fact, lies mainly in his influence on these and later artists (such as Johann Liss and Pieter Lastman, Rembrandt's teacher) who came to Italy from Germany and the Netherlands.

Self-portrait
Florence, Uffizi

HIS WORKS INCLUDE

St. Lawrence Prepared for Martyrdom, about 1600
London, N. G.

St. Paul on Malta, about 1600
London, N. G.

The Flight into Egypt, 1609
Munich, Alte Pin.

See also pages 98, 124

The Flight into Egypt (detail) 1609
Munich, Alte Pin.

Tobias and the Angel (detail)
London, N. G.

GREGOR ERHART

died 1540

A sculptor who relinquished late Gothic in favor of Renaissance values

Gregor Erhart was born probably at Ulm, the son of Ulm's best sculptor at that time, Michael Erhart. It was in his father's workshop that he learned the careful craftsmanship that marked everything he did. In 1493-94 he was collaborating with his father on the painted and gilded sculpture of an altarpiece for Blaubeuren Church in Bavaria. He then moved to Augsburg, at that time in its heyday as an art center and the home of the painters Hans Holbein the Elder and Hans Burgkmair. Four years later, already married, and in possession of a workshop and apprentices, Erhart had embarked on what was to be a career of lifelong success. He died in Augsburg in 1540.

Following in the steps of his father, who had once collaborated on an altarpiece with the elder Holbein, he carved *The Madonna of Mercy*, 1502, as the central figure of a folding shrine for which Holbein painted the wings. Erhart found patrons in Emperor Maximilian I, a great amateur of the arts, and the wealthy Fugger family of Augsburg. In a second *Madonna of Mercy*, about 1515, a portrait of the emperor is seen in one of the kneeling figures protected by the Madonna.

In the dozen or so years that separate the two *Madonnas* Erhart's style expanded and matured. The earlier figure is in the late Gothic tradition, with little hint of any knowledge of the forms of the Renaissance. The people protected by the Madonna are huddled inside her cloak in tight, narrow groups. The later version is broader, freer, and more effectively indicates the presence of a human body beneath ampler folds of drapery. A new Renaissance realism is also apparent in Erhart's magnificent nude figure of St. Mary Magdalen, about 1525.

The Madonna of Mercy, 1502
West Berlin, Staatl. Mus.

HIS WORKS INCLUDE

High Altarpiece, 1494
Blaubeuren, Monastery Church

The Madonna of Mercy, 1502
West Berlin, Staatl. Mus.

The Madonna of Mercy, about 1515
Frauenstein, Austria, Parish Church

St. Mary Magdalen, about 1525
Paris, Louvre

See also page 137

ANSELM FEUERBACH

1829-1880

A painter of portraits and mythological pictures with an intellectual and aesthetic flavor

Anselm Feuerbach was born in 1829 at Speyer, on the Rhine, into a learned family. His father was a professor of archeology, an uncle the well-known philosopher Ludwig Feuerbach.

In 1845 Feuerbach entered the Düsseldorf Academy, where he studied under the painter Wilhelm von Schadow. Afterwards, he went to Munich and Paris. The successive influences of two contemporaries in Paris, the anti-academic Gustave Courbet and the academician Thomas Couture, resulted first in his robust *Hafiz Outside the Tavern*, 1852, and then in his academic *Death of Aretino*, 1854.

In 1855, Feuerbach went to Italy on a salary from the prince regent, Friedrich of Baden, first to Venice and then to Rome, where he settled in 1856. In Venice he painted a large allegorical work, *Poetry*, to celebrate the prince regent's marriage. But it was coolly received, and Feuerbach was offended.

It was as a portrait painter that he achieved his finest results, which include numerous representations of his model, Nanna Risi. In the outstanding *Nanna* of

Self-portrait (detail)
East Berlin, Staatl. Mus.

HIS WORKS INCLUDE

Hafiz Outside the Tavern, 1852
Mannheim, Kunsthalle

Nanna, 1861
West Berlin, Staatl. Mus.

Iphigenia, 1871
Stuttgart, Staatsgal.

The Repast at the House of Plato, 1869
Karlsruhe, Kunsthalle

See also page 111

1861 the idealism of the original conception is enhanced by an air of serenity and a pose so tranquil that it is almost statuesque.

In 1873, Feuerbach became a professor at the Vienna Academy and painted *The Fall of the Titans* for the ceiling of its main hall. Three years later he returned to Venice, where he died in 1880.

GEORG FLEGEL   1566-1638

The first German painter to devote himself to still-life

Georg Flegel was born in 1566 in Bohemia, probably at Olmütz. By 1594 he was living in Frankfurt, where three years later he sought citizenship for himself and his wife. His sponsor on this occasion was the painter Lucas van Valkenborch, who apparently employed Flegel as his assistant on the still-lifes in his landscapes.

About 1600, however, Flegel established himself on his own. In 1611 the agent of Duke Philipp II of Pommern-Stettin sent his master a consignment of works of art that included a "fine likeness of a breakfast table, painted by Flegel." This piece was obviously more complicated than a simple arrangement of fruit or flowers, although the price, with frame, was only 18 florins. For the manuscript prayerbook of Duke Albrecht V of Bavaria, Flegel painted floral border decorations, exquisitely designed to harmonize with the script.

His early paintings were loosely constructed groups of comparatively few objects set on a tabletop and often interspersed with tiny insects and animals. His drawing was meticulous and the flowers and animals carefully studied. His later compositions were richer and more intricate, built up on diagonal lines in a manner already characteristic of the Baroque.

In 1627 Flegel was employing an assistant, one indication that, had the German interest in still-life not been arrested by the religious wars, he might have been the founder of a flourishing school. Among the treasures of the great collector Archduke Leopold Wilhelm 20 years after Flegel's death were 12 small still-lifes of fruit by him, all of equal size and in identical frames, clearly intended as a series.

Border Decoration of the *Prayerbook* of Duke Albrecht V of Bavaria
Munich, Bayerisches Nationalmus.

Still-life (detail) 1637
Frankfurt-am-Main, Historisches Mus.

HIS WORKS INCLUDE

Larder Lit by a Candle, about 1630-35
Karlsruhe, Kunsthalle

Still-life, 1637
Frankfurt-am-Main, Historisches Mus.

See also page 97

33

FRANCONIA, JONAS AND HOSEA
THURINGIA, ECKEHART AND UTA

about 1235
about 1250-60

German cathedral sculptures

The present cathedral of Bamberg in Franconia was erected between 1219 and 1237 by four successive companies of builders, a single sculptors' workshop being attached throughout the period. However, the master masons in charge of the sculpture program within and without the cathedral changed as the work progressed, so that it falls into two distinct phases. Up till about 1235 the hand of one outstanding anonymous sculptor can be seen. He was responsible in particular for the east choir screen, which he decorated with pairs of prophets and apostles, including Jonas and Hosea, in animated conversation with each other. He gave their gestures far greater freedom than was customary in the late Romanesque period, and despite the similarity of their heads, which appear to be derived from one and the same model, he portrayed each of them as an individual of different temperament.

This artist was probably still active when the sculptors of the second phase took the lead, which they did not relinquish until some years after the completion of the cathedral. They worked in a new style influenced by French cathedral sculpture —the Gothic. One of them made *The Bamberg Rider*, about 1237, the purest visual embodiment of 13th-century chivalry in Germany.

The height of this Gothic phase can be seen in the sculptures at the cathedral of Naumburg in Thuringia, where, in 1249, Bishop Dietrich of Wettin decided to add a west choir modeled on the choir at Bamberg. The master mason to whom the project was entrusted can be traced from his training in the workshops of northern France to his mature work, which includes his work at Naumburg and a poignant bandaged head, from the rood screen of Mainz Cathedral. In Naumburg he made a series of life size male and female standing figures to represent donors and patrons of the cathedral, many of them members of the House of Wettin and ancestors of Bishop Dietrich. His forceful and broad treatment of the stone and the strikingly varied expressions of the figures show the artist on the threshold of a new, realistic age. Among the different types and characters, Eckehart of Meissen, the sturdy country nobleman, contrasts effectively with his wife Uta, the embodiment of aristocratic refinement and one of the most beautiful figures in the series.

Jonas and Hosea (detail) about 1235
Bamberg, Cath.

Eckehart (detail) about 1250-60
Naumburg, Cath.

See also pages 132, 133

HIS WORKS INCLUDE

The Cross on the Mountaintop, 1807
Dresden, Gemäldegal.

The Forest, 1814
Hamburg, Kunsthalle

Two Men Contemplating
the Moon, 1819
Dresden, Gemäldegal.

See also page 105

CASPAR DAVID FRIEDRICH

1774-1840

The central figure in German Romantic landscape painting

Caspar David Friedrich was born in 1774 in the Baltic port of Greifswald in Pomerania. At 20 Friedrich went to Copenhagen. After studying for four years at the academy there, he returned to Germany and settled permanently in Dresden, at that time a thriving center of Romanticism in both literature and art. He joined the circle of poets around Tieck and Novalis and became friends with Philipp

Runge. In 1805 Friedrich won a prize for two sepia drawings in a competition sponsored by Goethe, whom he visited at Jena in 1811.

Friedrich's reputation rose. He was elected to the Berlin Academy in 1810 and the Dresden Academy in 1816. He married a Dresden girl and in 1820 shared a house with the Norwegian landscape painter J. C. C. Dahl. Friedrich often left Dresden on painting trips to the Baltic region and the Harz mountains. He also went back many times to visit his home town, Greifswald. The vast, flat expanse of the Pomeranian landscape and the somber mood it evoked remained a source of inspiration. Toward the end of his life an inborn melancholy strain in his nature took on such proportions that he was unable to work. After a stroke in 1835, he suffered from black depression until his death in 1840.

In Friedrich's first important painting, *The Cross on the Mountaintop*, 1807, there is already something of his highly personal approach to landscape. Although his paintings generally had their roots in real scenery, his main object was not to produce a naturalistic rendering of details, but to convey to the canvas a part of his own cosmic feeling for nature, his religious sense of the infinite. A thoughtful sadness underlies his views of the Harz mountains as well as *The Forest*, 1814. In order to emphasize a particular mood he often inserted human figures, perhaps seen from behind and absorbed in the contemplation of a stormy sunset or moonlight on the sea. But whether or not it contained figures, every landscape by Friedrich was an attempt in the Romantic manner to mirror a human experience in nature.

Woman at the Window, 1818
West Berlin, Staatl. Mus.

HANS BALDUNG, called GRIEN   1484/85-1545

An imaginative Strasbourg painter, draftsman, and designer of woodcuts and stained-glass windows

Hans Baldung, called Grien, was born in 1484 or 1485 at Weyersheim in Alsace, into a family of doctors and lawyers. His works, especially his woodcut designs, show that his main early influence was Albrecht Dürer, in whose studio he almost certainly worked while staying in Nuremberg from the age of about 17 to 22. In 1509 he became a citizen of Strasbourg and opened a prosperous workshop there. In the next year he married. His greatest output of woodcuts was between 1510 and 1523, when books containing his designs were published yearly in Strasbourg.

In 1512 Baldung moved to Freiburg to begin what was to be his masterpiece, a large folding high altar commissioned the previous year for the cathedral. Although it was finished in 1516, he stayed on at Freiburg busy with commissions for smaller religious panels, designs for stained-glass windows in the cathedral, and portraits. He also drew and painted a number of erotic, allegorical, or *memento mori* scenes, in which his favorite subject, the female nude, was sometimes gruesomely contrasted with the figure of death. An example is his effective *Death Kissing a Maiden*.

At the end of 1517, at the height of his fame, Baldung returned to Strasbourg,

Portrait of Caspar Hedion
Karlsruhe, Kunsthalle

where he remained until his death in 1545, rich, successful, and highly esteemed. In 1521 Jean Pellerin, the French art theorist, included Hans Grien of Strasbourg among the most famous painters of his day, next to Dürer, Cranach, and Holbein. Many of Baldung's religious works in Strasbourg were destroyed between 1525 and 1530 during the fury of the Reformation, and in his last years commissions for such paintings were few.

He painted at first in the late Gothic style, His manner then expanded and relaxed under the influence of Netherlandish and Italian pictures, which he must have seen in Germany. Finally, his style progressed toward the mannerism, the more complicated motion, the elongated figures, of late works such as *The Adoration of the Magi*, 1539, or *Noli Me Tangere*. Baldung's characteristically full, swelling female nudes of about 1517 also changed to more sophisticated, sinuous forms, like those of *The Three Graces*, about 1540.

Self-portrait
Erlangen, Universitätsbibl.

MATHIS GOTHARDT, called GRÜNEWALD   about 1470/80-1528

A great master of expression

The source of the name Grünewald is obscure. It first occurs about 150 years after the death of the artist, in the biography of him by the painter and writer Joachim von Sandrart. The discovery of his real name is a piece of modern detection, going back to 1917 when documents that mentioned a "Master Mathis" of Würzburg were found. They were soon recognized to refer to the painter who had hitherto been known only as Grünewald. Bit by bit, other documents referring either to Mathis Gothardt or Mathis Gothart-Neithardt or Mathis Neithardt were pieced together, until it became possible to establish a sketchy biography. It is assumed that the artist's original name was Gothardt, and that he thought it prudent to add the Neithardt when he married a widow of that name and adopted her young son.

Grünewald was born probably at Würzburg, between 1470 and 1480. By 1501 he had established himself at Seligenstadt, running a large workshop for wood-carvers and painters that continued to flourish until he left the town 25 years later. Evidently he prospered. He bought more than one house in Seligenstadt and owned other property there besides. Moreover, he was drawing a salary by virtue of his appointment in 1508 as court painter to the archbishop-elector of Mainz. When the elector died in 1514, Grünewald was still in his employ. Probably he then became court painter to the new elector, Cardinal Albrecht of Hohenzollern, but in any case he was in the cardinal's service from 1516 to 1526. At least two of Grünewald's surviving works were painted for Cardinal Albrecht: the panel *The Dead Christ*, which bears the cardinal's coat of arms, and *The Disputation of St. Erasmus and St. Maurice*, in which St. Erasmus is a portrait of the cardinal himself.

An important subsidiary office at the court of the electors was that of supervisor of works. In this capacity Grünewald was responsible for the rebuilding of the palace at Aschaffenburg about 1511 and probably had a similar charge over Cardinal Albrecht's new buildings at Halle. His work for other patrons includes his masterpiece, a huge folding altar commissioned by Guido Gersi, the Italian preceptor of the Antonite monastery at Isenheim, intended to provide a suitable setting for a carved shrine already in the monks' possession.

Grünewald's Lutheran sympathies may have involved him in the peasant rising of 1525. Whatever the reason, he left Seligenstadt in 1526 to move to Frankfurt and later Halle, whose Protestant magistrate gave him employment as a hydraulic engineer. It is thought that he painted nothing after he left Seligenstadt. He died at Halle in 1528.

When Grünewald is compared with Albrecht Dürer (1471-1528), his exact contemporary, the two painters are to be seen standing at opposite poles of German art. However, like Dürer, Grünewald was aware of recent trends in Italian painting. *The Isenheim Altarpiece*, Grünewald's most important work, shows a mastery of perspective, anatomy, and drapery that clearly has its closest parallel in Renaissance Italy. But unlike Dürer's, Grünewald's vision was firmly rooted in the Gothic tradition. In *The Isenheim Altarpiece* again, there are fantastic landscapes and monsters that may well be taken as proof of his familiarity with the medieval idiom

HIS WORKS INCLUDE

The Mocking of Christ, 1503
Munich, Alte Pin.

The Small Crucifixion, about 1505-10
*Washington, D. C., N. G.
Samuel H. Kress Coll.*

The Isenheim Altarpiece, about 1505-15
Colmar, France, Mus.

The Virgin and Child, 1517-20
Stuppach, Parish Church

The Crucifixion, about 1524
Karlsruhe, Kunsthalle

The Disputation of St. Erasmus and St. Maurice, about 1525
Munich, Alte Pin.

See also pages 91, 148

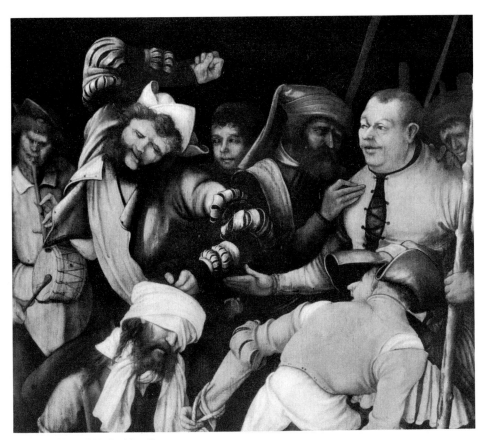

The Mocking of Christ (detail) 1503
Munich, Alte Pin.

St. Elizabeth of Hungary, about 1512
Donaueschingen, Fürstenbergische Gal.

of the Netherlandish painter Hieronymus Bosch. Grünewald's fervent emotion and iridescent, expressive colors are entirely his, however, and unique in German painting.

The amalgamation of Italian Renaissance forms with an inherently anticlassical spirit was bound to set up tensions. In *The Isenheim Altarpiece* these take shape in strange juxtapositions of the visionary and ethereal with raw reality: the tortured figure of Christ in the Crucifixion panel, for example, as compared to the kneeling Virgin accompanied by a host of music-making angels in the so-called Christmas panel. One source of some of these unusual contrasts was the 14th-century "Revelations of St. Bridget of Sweden." Grünewald's crucified Christ was thus intended to interpret St. Bridget's words: "His feet were curled around the nails, as around door hinges," while the mystic kneeling Virgin of the Christmas panel was inspired by St. Bridget's "Maria Aeterna decreed by God before the Creation to be the Mother of God."

There are a few drawings by Grünewald, mostly detail studies for both lost and surviving works. They are consistent in style with his paintings. Their delicate, sensitive line and superb lighting and shading seem to have captured the first inspiration of each composition.

J. K. Huysmans Grünewald—the Paintings London, 1958

St. Lucy, about 1512
Donaueschingen, Fürstenbergische Gal.

The Disputation of St. Erasmus and St. Maurice (detail) about 1525
Munich, Alte Pin.

MATTHÄUS GÜNTHER

1705-1788

A South German master of Rococo

Matthäus Günther was born in 1705, in Unterpeissenburg near Wessobrunn, Bavaria. He was probably educated in Wessobrunn, then a center of fresco painting. Afterwards he went to Munich, where he was taken into the workshop of the well-known painter, Cosmas Damian Asam. For five years, Günther was almost certainly Asam's assistant and collaborator on big fresco commissions. In 1731 he moved to Augsburg, where he married and as a master painter set up a workshop of his own. In accordance with the contemporary custom, he spent his summers in various places painting fresco cycles, and his winters in the Augsburg studio working on altarpieces and the oil sketches for the fresco commissions of the following season.

At first, as in his early frescoes, 1733, at Sterzing in the Tyrol, Günther's painted architectural settings were a little overweight. But soon, as he lightened his coloring to a range of silvery tones, both his architecture and the figures it surrounded grew more ethereal and assumed the true Rococo spirit. Toward the end of the 1740's he frequently dispensed altogether with the architectural framework in favor of an asymmetrical composition. It was at this time that he did some work in Amorbach, and was able to study at first hand recent paintings by the greatest Italian master of Rococo, Giovanni Battista Tiepolo. The experience made his own conceptions airier, lighter, and more colorful.

Despite formidable competition from other representatives of the flourishing South German school, commissions flowed steadily into Günther's workshop. They came from the great monasteries of Bavaria and Swabia, as well as from the wealthiest and most distinguished individual patrons. Günther was appointed co-director of the Augsburg Academy in 1762 and kept the post for 22 years. He died in 1788, two years after the death of his only son.

Fresco (detail): from The Aeneas Cycle
1757
Stuttgart, Neues Schloss

HIS WORKS INCLUDE

Frescoes, 1733
Sterzing, Tyrol, Deutschorden Church

Frescoes, 1745-47
Amorbach, Church

The Aeneas Cycle (frescoes) 1757
Stuttgart, Neues Schloss

Frescoes, 1760
Aldersbach, Bavaria, Monastery Library,

See also page 102

HANS HOLBEIN the YOUNGER

1497/98-1543

A portrait painter of international renown even in his own lifetime

Hans Holbein the Younger was born in Augsburg in 1497 or 1498. His father, Hans Holbein the Elder, was a distinguished painter in the Late Gothic style, with a busy workshop in which he gave his two sons, Ambrosius and Hans, a thorough technical grounding.

Before 1514, however, the workshop closed down. The brothers made their way to Switzerland and apprenticed themselves to a painter in Basel. Hans Holbein's excellence as a draftsman was already conspicuous. Soon it created a demand for his illustrations among the Basel publishers. It was probably through one of them,

Self-portrait
Florence, Uffizi

Erasmus of Rotterdam, 1523
Paris, Louvre

Froben, that the Holbeins met the learned, witty and caustic Erasmus of Rotterdam, for an edition of whose book "The Praise of Folly," 1509, they prepared marginal drawings together.

In 1517 Hans Holbein went to Lucerne. There he was asked to decorate the façade and interior of the Hertenstein house, of which only a small fragment now remains. He was still away when his brother Ambrosius died in Basel in 1519. After his return he became a citizen of Basel and a member of the painters' guild, with a workshop of his own. He married Elizabeth Binzenstock, who in 1522 posed with their infant son Philipp for his *Solothurn Virgin and Child*, 1522. But the marriage was clearly not a happy one. When Holbein went abroad, even for several years at a time, he went alone.

He had already toured northern Italy, absorbing the atmosphere of the Renaissance and, in particular, the example of Leonardo. In 1520 he painted a panel

Portrait of a Young Woman,
about 1530
The Hague, Mauritshuis

The Ambassadors, 1533
London, N. G.

after the first great work of the High Renaissance, Leonardo's mural of *The Last Supper*, in Milan. In 1523 to 1524 he traveled in France, where he achieved immediate popular success in Lyons with the publication of his woodcuts of *The Dance of Death*. His contact with the Italian and the French Renaissance took him far beyond the boundaries of Late Gothic art observed in his father's studio, into a new dimension created by a new sense of space and mass. Nevertheless, the basis of his portraits was still the extraordinary insight into character that his father had cultivated in him from the first. His art, possessing all the awareness of the detached observer, was international.

The flow of commissions for portraits and religious, monumental, and decorative works was increasing. Holbein's circle of friends and regular patrons grew with it. For his friend Jakob Meyer, burgomaster of Basel, he painted family portraits in 1517 and 1528. But his fame as a portraitist was first established throughout Europe by three portraits of Erasmus done in 1523. About this time Holbein also illustrated Luther's Bible. In 1521 he had started on frescoes commissioned from him for the new council chamber of the Basel Town Hall. But repercussions of the Reformation were causing chaos in Basel, and his work was intermittent. Finally, his career was so seriously threatened that in 1526 he went to London. On the way he met the Flemish painter Quentin Massys in Antwerp.

Holbein brought to England an introduction from Erasmus to his friend Sir Thomas More, with whom he stayed for some time. More was already living in semi-retirement, and Erasmus' friends in general were out of favor with King Henry VIII. But even though Holbein did not appear at the English court, the portraits from this first stay in England are among his best works. He painted Sir Thomas More and his family, Archbishop Warham, the royal astronomer Nikolaus Kratzer, and other distinguished sitters.

In 1528 he went back to Basel. Despite the efforts of the town council to keep him there, the continuing religious upheavals disturbed him as much as before, and he settled permanently in London in 1532. There he worked for several years on a long succession of portrait commissions for German merchants, starting with his brilliant portrait of the Hanseatic merchant Georg Gisze. In 1533 he painted Thomas Cromwell, at that time high in King Henry's esteem. It was possibly through Cromwell that he at last got an introduction to the court. This in turn obtained him an appointment as court painter to Henry VIII, a studio in the tower of Whitehall Palace, and a salary of £20 a year. He was employed on royal portraits, miniatures, interior decorations, and designs for jewelry, for state robes, and for table silver. He was attached to delegations sent abroad to negotiate marriages for the king, as portrait painter of the prospective brides.

From then on Holbein was so overwhelmed with commissions that he no longer had time to work from the model, but was forced instead to make a series of concise sketches of his sitter, which he could work up later into the portrait. His 150 portraits were only part of his output during the 11 years between 1532 and his death from the plague in 1543.

P. Ganz Holbein London, 1950

The Duke of Norfolk (detail)
about 1539
Windsor, England, Royal Coll.

HH

HIS WORKS INCLUDE

Signboard for a Schoolmaster, 1516
Basel, Kunstmus.

The Last Supper, 1520
Basel, Kunstmus.

Murals of the Council Chamber of the Basel Town Hall, 1521-31
Basel, Kunstmus.

Portrait of Sir Thomas More, 1527
New York, Frick Coll.

The Artist's Family, about 1529
Basel, Kunstmus.

Portrait of Thomas Cromwell, 1533
New York, Frick Coll.

See also pages 94, 119, 121

41

WOLF HUBER

about 1490-1553

A landscapist, portrait painter, and draftsman of the Danube School

Wolf Huber was born about 1490 in the mountain town of Feldkirch in Austria and spent the greater part of his life in Passau, on the Danube River near the Austrian border of Germany. The early contact with his contemporary Albrecht Altdorfer, and perhaps with other Danube masters, is apparent from his work. Like them, he devoted his energies chiefly to landscape.

Huber was at his best in pure landscape drawings, of which the earliest known is *The Mondsee* of 1510. It was shortly after this date that he moved to Passau, to become court painter to Duke Ernst and, in time, to his successor. Both patrons gave him their protection against the hostility of the Passau Painters' Guild, which he did not have to join as he was court painter. Eventually he became a citizen of Passau and master mason to the town. Various records relate his orders to examine buildings and make estimates for the town council. In 1539 he and his wife purchased a building site from the cathedral chapter of Passau. Meanwhile, he seems to have been careful to maintain his ties with his home town, Feldkirch. Of two altarpiece commissions that he received in 1515 from the Feldkirch Confraternity of St. Anne, one was completed and delivered by 1521. Huber died in 1553 in Passau, an honored citizen.

Huber's oil paintings, both landscapes and portraits, necessitated preliminary drawings. His painting style featured square heads, squat figures, and slightly contorted, mannered poses, and showed small feeling for plastic form and little warmth of expression. On the other hand, his drawings and watercolors, whether preliminary studies or not, are always of great lyrical charm. The landscape drawings in particular, popular and copied even during his lifetime, are products of his fully "romantic" response to the poetry of nature.

Self-portrait, 1522
West Berlin, Staatl. Mus.

HIS WORKS INCLUDE

Man with a Cap, about 1522
West Berlin, Staatl. Mus.

Portrait of a Man, 1522
Basel, Kunstmus.

The Raising of the Cross, about 1525
Vienna, Kunsthist. Mus.

Jakob Ziegler, 1544-49
Vienna, Kunsthist. Mus.

See also page 119

The Flight into Egypt (detail) about 1530
West Berlin, Staatl. Mus.

42

INNSBRUCK: THE TOMB OF MAXIMILIAN I   about 1509-93

A monument in the Italian Renaissance manner

The monument of Emperor Maximilian is situated in a Renaissance-style Franciscan church (Hofkirche) in Innsbruck, erected from 1553 to 1563 in compliance with the will of Emperor Maximilian I for the purpose of enshrining his monument. The massive marble sarcophogus occupies the center of the nave, and Maximilian is represented in a kneeling position, in bronze on the sarcaphogus. An impressive array of 28 bronze life-size statues of ancient heroes and of Maximilian's contemporaries in the guise of mourners and torchbearers surround his figure.

The general design of the monument was created by Gilg Sesselschreiber of Augsburg, the court painter, and the figure of Maximilian by L. del Duca. Some of the other sculptors were Stephan Godl, Bernhard Godl, Gregor Löffler, Hans Leinberger, and Peter Vischer. Vischer's statue of King Arthur stands out as the most brilliant. The vigorous lines, the noble features, and the exquisite finish of detail on his armor are fused into a statue worthy of the flower of chivalry. In contrast to the legendary Arthur is Leinberger's Count Albrecht of Hapsburg, whose clenched fist and courtier's pose represent the graceful dignity of the aristocrat.

There are 24 reliefs in marble, representing the principal events in the emperor's life. Many of the heads are portraits; the features of Maximilian at different periods of life are unmistakable, and the characteristics of different nationalities are faithfully rendered.

C. Headlan   Peter Vischer   London, 1901

Count Albrecht of Hapsburg, 1518:
from the Tomb of Emperor
Maximilian I
Innsbruck, Hofkirche

See also page 139

JOSEPH ANTON KOCH   1768-1839

An Austrian painter of mountain scenery

Joseph Anton Koch was born in 1768, the son of poor peasants, in Obergiblern in the Austrian Tyrol. As a boy he practiced drawing while he watched the sheep. At the age of 16 he began his first serious training in Augsburg. After a year he went to school in Stuttgart, but although he won prizes, he was not amenable to discipline. In 1791 he broke away altogether, to lead an adventurous, irregular life for the next few years.

From 1792 to 1794 he lived in the Swiss Alps, making continuous studies of the Alpine scenery. A walking tour to Italy brought him to Rome in 1795. He made many friends among the foreign artists resident there, and shared a house with the Danish Neoclassic sculptor, Bertel Thorwaldsen.

After about eight years in Rome, Koch sold an oil painting to a titled German who admired his work. This won him an introduction to the circle of German aris-

HIS WORKS INCLUDE

The Bernese Oberland, 1815
Vienna, Österreichische Gal.

Four frescoes, 1825-29
Rome, Casa Massimo, Dante Room

Noah's Thankoffering, about 1815
West Berlin, Staatl. Mus.

See also page 107

The Schmadribach Fall (detail) 1821-22
Munich, Alte Pin.

tocrats and art connoisseurs living in Rome. In 1812 he returned with his Italian wife and family to Austria. The three years that he spent in Vienna were among his most successful, but neither he nor his wife could settle down. Back in Rome in 1815, Koch was welcomed by friends and colleagues alike.

Meanwhile his painting matured. In moderate-sized landscapes with figures, he presented the grandeur of mountains, rocks, waterfalls, and gorges in a monumental way, stressing the crystalline structure of the stone rather than the organic world of trees and plants. The impressive over-all effect was heightened by clear, cold lighting and pale color.

In 1811 Koch's *Subiaco* was acclaimed at a Munich exhibition. But his art did not usually attract customers, and he found it more and more difficult to make a living. He received one important commission in 1825, to finish Philipp Veit's decorations in the Dante room of the Casa Massimo in Rome. Assisted by Julius Schnorr von Carolsfeld, he painted four large frescoes for this by 1829. Eventually his financial troubles assumed serious proportions. His friends obtained a pension from Vienna for him. It was too late to save his health, and he died soon afterwards.

Macbeth and the Witches, 1835
Innsbruck, Landesmus.

View of Oleveno
Munich, Alte Pin.

WILHELM LEIBL   1844-1900

A portraitist and genre painter

W. Leibl.

HIS WORKS INCLUDE

Cocotte, 1869
Cologne, Wallraf-Richartz-Mus.

Old Parisienne, 1870
Cologne, Wallraf-Richartz-Mus.

Women of Dachau, 1875
West Berlin, Staatl. Mus.

See also page 112

Wilhelm Leibl was born on October 23, 1844, in Cologne, where his father was director of music at Cologne Cathedral. In 1861 he began to study under a local painter and three years later went to the Munich Academy. Between 1866 and 1869 he made further studies under two different painters. He then exhibited for the first time in Munich. His early work was heavily influenced by Dutch painting. He chose everyday subjects, which he treated entirely without the sentiment and romanticism typical of contemporary German art,

44

From 1869 until nine months later, Leibl lived in Paris, working with Gustave Courbet and thus strengthening his attachment to realism. The Franco-Prussian War made it necessary for him to return to Germany. In 1870 he was awarded the Paris gold medal for his *Portrait of Frau Gedon*, in which Rembrandt's influence is clearly discernible.

He stayed in Munich from 1870 to 1873, then at various small villages in Bavaria, living in the same way as his peasant neighbors and painting the scenes around him. He still viewed his subjects with great matter-of-factness; no detail escaped his careful, perfect draftsmanship. This element of his mature work was to influence the New Objectivists of the 1920's, their figure studies and portrait drawing in particular.

From 1878 to 1881 Leibl made his home in the little Bavarian town of Berbling, where he painted *Three Women in Church*. He moved to Aibling and then, in 1892, to Kutterling. He died in Würzburg on December 4, 1900. Although his subjects remained free to the end from any trace of romantic idealism, Dutch art failed to retain its hold on him in his later years. He then achieved a kind of personal impressionism, characterized by a stronger and broader though always delicate technique and a more direct use of color.

Self-portrait, 1896
Cologne, Wallraf-Richartz-Mus.

JOHANN LISS
about 1597-1629/30

An early Baroque painter who died in Italy in mid-career

Johann Liss was born toward the end of the 16th century at Oldenburg in Schleswig-Holstein. He went to the Netherlands to be trained as a painter and then journeyed to Italy. Having spent some months in Rome, he settled in 1621 in Venice, where, only eight years later, he died of the plague.

Liss' early death cut short one of the most promising careers among early German Baroque artists. Although most of his output belongs to the eleven years between 1618 and 1629 it constitutes a valuable contribution to Venetian as well as to German painting of the 17th century.

Almost immediately after Liss reached Rome, the down-to-earth realism that he had learned in the Netherlands, very clear in his early work and still apparent in 1620 in *The Morra Players* and *Judith and Holofernes*, changed into a more sophisticated, elegant Italianate manner. But the Netherlandish influence by no means disappeared. Liss' realist tendency, kept alive in Rome by the example of works by Caravaggio, was responsible for the freshness, robustness, and spontaneity that underlay his style to the last. It was these qualities that finally brought him his reputation as one of the strongest and most progressive artists produced by 17th-century Germany. The treatment of some of his mythological subjects, in decorative compositions full of color and light, foreshadows the Baroque style of a century later. Liss remained in almost total oblivion for a long time after his death, and has only been rediscovered in the 20th century.

Judith and Holofernes, 1620
London, N. G.

Lis

HIS WORKS INCLUDE
The Quack, about 1617
Bremen, Kunsthalle

Judith and Holofernes, 1620
London, N. G.

See also page 99

The Madonna of the Rose Bower
Cologne, Wallraf-Richartz-Mus.

STEFAN LOCHNER
about 1400-1451

A Cologne painter who made the final exquisite distillation of the Soft Style

Stefan Lochner was born about 1400, in Meersburg. He seems to have traveled and studied in the Netherlands and France before he settled in Cologne for the rest of his life. In 1442 he was commissioned by the Cologne Council to paint the city coat of arms on a barrel of wine to be presented to King Friedrich III. In 1447 he was elected, and three years later re-elected, to the city council. Early in 1451 he had news of his parents' death in Meersburg, and later in the year he too died, probably of the plague, in Cologne.

No work by him is signed, but an entry in the diary kept by Dürer on his journey to the Netherlands in 1520 reveals Lochner's Christian name. Dürer relates that he paid two white pennies in Cologne to have the picture painted by "Master Stefan of Cologne" opened and shown to him. This was Lochner's masterpiece, *The Altar of the City Patrons*, commissioned by the city elders. The altarpiece is now in the cathedral and hence is often known as *The Cathedral Picture.*

This and other paintings assigned to Lochner establish him as a major representative of the Soft Style, a German branch of International Gothic. He looked back, to the previous exponents of the Soft Style in Cologne, rather than forward.

Other, perhaps earlier paintings of his, *The Last Judgment* and *St. Jerome in his Cell*, prove that he also knew something of recent trends in Flanders, France, and Burgundy, where the Master of Flémalle and Franco-Burgundian manuscript illuminators were working. In fact, the careful eye of the illuminator was so firmly implanted in Lochner that it controlled even his later work. By the time of *The Altar of the City Patrons*, he had added a new mastery of closely knit composition.

Thus Lochner first supplemented, then organized the lyricism that he found in the earlier masters of Cologne, restoring to his city, for the last time, a position of national artistic importance.

HIS WORKS INCLUDE

The Last Judgment
Cologne, Wallraf-Richartz-Mus.

The Presentation in the Temple, 1447
Darmstadt, Hessisches Landesmus.

The Madonna of the Rose Bower
Cologne, Wallraf-Richartz-Mus.

See also page 83

Self-portrait
Bern, Kunstmus.

NIKLAS MANUEL (DEUTSCH)
about 1484-1530

A Swiss draftsman, painter, poet, and politician

The artist Niklas Manuel was born in Bern, Switzerland, about 1484, and called Allemania. He used the German equivalent, Deutsch, of his surname only when putting his name to his pictures, which he signed "N. M. D."

Manuel probably began his career by designing stained glass, for two glass panels by him are dated about 1509. He married that year, and the youngest of his six children, Niklas Manuel II, acquired a reputation of his own as a stained-glass designer.

The elder Manuel's best work is from his drawings, in pen, chalk, charcoal, pastel, and silverpoint. But he was also a painter and poet, as well as a successful politician. He became a member of the council of Obergerbern in 1512, and a city councilor of Bern two years before he died there in 1530. A fervent reformer, he used both writing and drawing as vehicles for his satires of the Catholic clergy.

In 1516, and again in 1522, Manuel served as secretary of the Swiss mercenary troops known as the Lansquenets. He took part in their campaigns in Italy without having to fight, and his *Studies of Lansquenets* are among his best drawings.

Both of his best-known paintings, *The Judgment of Paris* and *The Beheading of John the Baptist*, contain fantastic female headdresses, which are characteristic of Manuel's gradual absorption of Renaissance elements into the Gothic style with which he had started. In his hands the combination resulted in a striking blend of sophistication and naïveté.

HIS WORKS INCLUDE

Death Embracing a Maiden, 1517
Basel, Kunstmus.

The Judgment of Paris, about 1523
Basel, Kunstmus.

The Beheading of John the Baptist,
about 1516
Bern, Kunstmus.

See also page 123

Pyramus and Thisbe (detail) 1529
Basel, Kunstmus.

MANUSCRIPT: ADA GOSPELS, ST. LUKE   about 800
MANUSCRIPT: REICHENAU, THE ANNUNCIATION
            TO THE SHEPHERDS   about 1007/12
MANUSCRIPT: COLOGNE, ST. PANTALEON   1170

Germanic book illuminations

The revival of art encouraged by Emperor Charlemagne around 800 was particularly fruitful in the field of book illumination. Illuminators were taught to look not only to splendors of the Early Christian period in Italy, but beyond to Near Eastern

See also pages 73, 74

St. Luke: from the Ada Gospels,
(detail) about 800
Trier, Stadtbibl.

models, such as Byzantine, Syrian or Armenian manuscripts. Too laborious to be widely practiced, the art of illumination was confined under Charlemagne and his successors to the main monasteries of France and Germany and to the imperial court itself.

One of the most famous of the sumptuous court manuscripts of the reign of Charlemagne is the Ada Gospels, written for Abbess Ada, by tradition the emperor's sister. The artist made lavish use of gold and silver and portrayed the evangelists as beardless young men in the Western manner, very different from the bearded, restrained Eastern patriarchs appearing in earlier illuminations.

Toward the end of the 9th century the quality of manuscript illumination declined in Germany, to be splendidly revived again in the 10th century under the Emperors Otto I, II, and III. In the Ottonian period, an influential school of illumination grew up in the great monastery of Reichenau Island in Lake Constance. The Reichenau style, characterized by austerely expressive linear rhythms, had attained a monumental grandeur by the turn of the century, as seen in the Pericope Book of Emperor Henry II. It was a monumental grandeur approaching that of contemporary wall painting, e.g., the frescoes still to be seen in one of the Reichenau churches.

Among other centers of Ottonian illumination was Cologne, whose vitality lasted well into the subsequent Romanesque period, 11th to late 12th century. A manuscript, about 1170, from the Cologne Monastery of St. Pantaleon is a fine example. In one full-page illumination St. Pantaleon stands against a blue background framed in green, colors reminiscent of the enamels favored by contemporary goldsmiths. The artist's conception of the human body emphasized outline, rather than movement or surface values, resulting in the abstract quality typical of the Romanesque style.

The Marriage at Cana (detail): from
The Buxtehude Altarpiece, about 1380
Hamburg, Kunsthalle

MASTER BERTRAM   about 1345-1414/15

The painter who put medieval Hamburg on the map of German art

Master Bertram was born about 1345 at Minden, Westphalia, but rose to a position of wealth and distinction in Hamburg. In 1367, at about the age of 22, he was a member of the Hamburg Painters' Guild.

It was Master Bertram who first raised Hamburg to the status of an art center. The artists of Lübeck, 35 miles away, had previously been busier and better known. Thus it is significant that when the Holy Roman Emperor, Charles IV, paid a state visit to Lübeck in 1375, Master Bertram of Hamburg was officially invited there for the occasion.

Four years later he painted his finest work, for the Church of St. Peter in Hamburg. This imposing altarpiece, set up in 1383, consists of sculptures of the saints and 24 panels depicting the Creation and the life of the Virgin. The panels bear similarities to the new, robust art successfully nurtured in Bohemia by Charles IV. It is thought that Master Bertram had been to Prague, to see for himself the paintings in the Chapel of the Holy Cross in the emperor's castle of Karlstein, since he did belong to the newly founded confraternity of the Holy Cross.

Master Bertram apparently ran a big workshop at Hamburg, through which he exercised his sway over the taste and the style of his contemporaries and immediate posterity. The most distinguished artist to be trained in his studio was undoubtedly the painter of *The Buxtehude Altarpiece*, about 1380, which had so much in common with the work of Master Bertram that it was once thought to be by him.

Toward the end of his life Master Bertram was a rich man. His will of 1410 mentions numerous bequests to monasteries and churches. He died in Hamburg in 1414 or 1415.

The Crucifixion:
from The Passion Altar, 1379
Hanover, Landesmus.

HIS WORKS INCLUDE

Altarpiece of the Creation and the
Life of the Virgin, 1379
Hamburg, Kunsthalle

The Passion Altar, 1379
Hanover, Landesmus.

See also page 77

MASTER E. S.   about 1420- about 1468

The first outstanding master of copperplate engraving in the modern sense

The anonymous engraver and goldsmith known as Master E. S. was born probably about 1420. He was once also called the Master of 1466, the date inscribed on one of his engravings, *The Virgin and Child of Einsiedeln*. As he made at least three versions of the Virgin of this Swiss town, it has been suggested that he was born in Switzerland. He died about 1468.

Many engravings and some drawings have been attributed to him. His subjects range from the Old and New Testaments, through saints and allegory to decorative designs that include playing cards and a figure alphabet.

His style was formed partly by the Netherlandish influence current in Germany at that time, but its chief sources were German and French, among them Konrad Witz and his circle, and Burgundian manuscript illuminators. Master E. S. in his turn combined and handed down these influences to the German painters and engravers of the end of the 15th century.

His earliest engravings, dating from about 1452, include *The Garden of Paradise*, which shows the Christ Child at His mother's feet, and *A Pair of Lovers*, depicting a couple on a grassy bank. The figures, drawn with great delicacy, are set in postures that suggest the Late Gothic fashion. At the end of Master E. S.'s life this stiff element in his work became pronounced to the point of exaggeration. His middle period is characterized by a much more powerful line and the particular emphasis given by tiny cross-hatchings. *The Annunciation* and *The Holy Night* are good examples of prints from this period.

The Virgin and Child of
Einsiedeln (detail) 1466   *engraving*
Dresden, Kupferstichkabinett, et al.

HIS WORKS INCLUDE

Engravings:

The Annunciation

The Garden of Paradise

A Pair of Lovers

Holy Night

St. Sebastian, 1467

See also page 114

The Adoration of the Magi, 1424
Hamburg, Kunsthalle

Altarpiece of St. Thomas of
Canterbury, after 1424
Hamburg, Kunsthalle

See also page 81

MASTER FRANCKE

active about 1405-after 1425

A master of the Soft Style

So little is known of the life of Master Francke, one of the greatest German painters of his day, that guesses as to his identity are still being made. It is known, however, that he lived and worked in Hamburg. He was engaged by the confraternity of Hamburg merchants who traded with England to paint an altarpiece, dedicated to St. Thomas of Canterbury, for their chapel in the Church of St. Johann.

In some paintings by Master Francke, particularly the early St. Barbara altarpiece, his style so closely approaches that of the contemporary manuscript illuminations of northern France—*The Hours of Marshal Boucicaut* or *The Wonders of the World*—that he must have visited France about 1405. Later he found a delicate style of his own, which was one source of the Soft Style then flooding German art. Master Francke's drawing is firm, rhythmical, even lyrical; his coloring is warm. The feeling for space in some of his landscape settings is so well defined that even his red, starpatterned backdrops can scarcely make them seem unreal.

St. Barbara Altarpiece (detail) 1420
Helsinki, Finland, Nat. Mus.

The Scourging, about 1425
Hamburg, Kunsthalle

The Scourging (detail) about 1425
Hamburg, Kunsthalle

Altarpiece of St. Thomas, about 1500
Cologne, Wallraf-Richartz-Mus.

The Crucifixion: center panel of an
altarpiece, about 1500
Cologne, Wallraf-Richartz-Mus.

Altarpiece of St. Bartholomew,
about 1510
Munich, Alte Pin.

See also page 86

MASTER OF THE
ST. BARTHOLOMEW ALTARPIECE

active about 1470-1510

A Cologne painter who was a superb draftsman and colorist

This anonymous master is named after his chief work, the altarpiece of St. Bartholomew, which he painted for the Cologne Church of St. Columba. His two other major altarpieces, those of St. Thomas and of The Crucifixion, were executed about 1500 for the Carthusian Monastery of Cologne.

Born possibly in Holland, the Master of St. Bartholomew worked during approximately the decade of the 1470's in the Netherlands and shortly afterwards in Cologne, where all his best work was commissioned by churches. The considerable group of paintings attributed to him proves him to be an important representative of the Late Gothic style. His early products are tinged with a Netherlandish influence, and in the paintings subsequent to his return to Cologne the local tradition has left its softening, sweetening mark. Yet his art was very individual.

He had a feeling for brilliant color, using glazes to give his pigments a transparent luster. He also had a consistent meticulousness, most notable in the sharp precision of his contours and details of costume. The dancing stance, the elegant, almost mannered posturing of his figures have caused the Master of St. Bartholomew to be called the "Crivelli of the North." Particularly characteristic of him are the long, spidery fingers that he delighted to paint.

Altarpiece of St. Bartholomew: center panel, about 1510 *Munich, Alte Pin.*

MASTER OF ST. VERONICA   active about 1400-1440

A Cologne painter in the Soft Style

This anonymous Cologne painter was active during the first part of the 15th century. Like his contemporary, the Master of the Upper Rhine, he was one of the finest representatives of the branch of International Gothic that is known as the Soft Style. The master of St. Veronica is named after a panel originally painted for the Cologne Church of St. Severin, and possibly intended to serve as the door of a reliquary shrine. Another work, *The Madonna and Child with a Pea Blossom*, is also generally ascribed to him. It is filled with the same lyrical charm and economical, yet rhythmical line.

A group of paintings by various anonymous painters in the immediate following of the Master of St. Veronica testifies to his influence in Cologne during the first decades of the 15th century. But this influence was by no means confined to Cologne. It can be traced in works of the Soft Style to Westphalia and beyond.

St. Veronica with the Holy Kerchief, (detail) about 1400   *Munich, Alte Pin.*

HIS WORKS INCLUDE
Scenes of the Passion
Cologne, Wallraf-Richartz-Mus.

See also page 80

MASTER OF THE UPPER RHINE   active about 1410-1420

An early painter in miniature

This anonymous master painted in the region of the upper Rhine in the early part of the 15th century. *The Garden of Paradise*, a panel no more than one foot across, is one of the most attractive works in the Soft Style, a German form of International Gothic. With minute precision the Virgin is shown seated in a walled garden with the Christ Child learning music at her feet. Male and female saints are at their tasks or talking informally on either side. Luxurious flowers, trees, and exotic birds

HIS WORKS INCLUDE
The Garden of Paradise, about 1410
Frankfurt-am-Main, Historisches Mus.

See also page 82

give the idyllic note appropriate to the scene. Thus, he is sometimes known as the Master of the Garden of Paradise.

Various other paintings have been attributed to the artist. He may also have been the author of a few woodcuts that depict the Madonna and Child, or the Child alone, in a lyrical manner very like that of *The Garden of Paradise*.

FRANZ ANTON MAULBERTSCH 1724-1796

One of the most original of all fresco painters

Self-portrait (detail)
Vienna, Österreichische Gal.

HIS WORKS INCLUDE

St. Walburga, 1749
Ulm, Parish Church

Frescoes, 1751-53
Vienna, Church of the Piarists

The Martyrdom of St. Jude and St. Simon. about 1760
Vienna, Österreichische Gal.

Frescoes, 1775
Innsbruck, Hofburg, Riesensaal

See also page 103

Franz Anton Maulbertsch was born in Langenargen, Swabia, in 1724. His first teacher was probably his father, a painter little known outside Langenargen, and it must have been apparent that the boy's talent demanded better instruction than he could get in the provinces.

At 15 Maulbertsch went to Vienna. He was at first apprenticed to a painter of mediocre ability, but his entrance the same year to the academy brought him into contact with Paul Troger and the other great decorative painters of his time.

In 1745 the academy had to close temporarily for either lack of funds or permanent quarters, but Maulbertsch was already qualified as a master painter. He married that year in the Cathedral of St. Stephen in Vienna, and doubtless set up a workshop of his own. He never lost touch with the academy. When it reopened in 1749, he resumed his student status there, winning first prize in the next year's competition for an *Allegory of the Fate of the Academy*. Only a small grisaille sketch for this painting, and a copy of it, remain. Maulbertsch was elected in 1759 to membership of the academy, and 11 years later to a professorship and a place on its council. He died in Vienna in 1796.

During an exceptionally busy life Maulbertsch painted fresco cycles in 59 diffe-

Study of Figures in Adoration (detail) 1764
Vienna, Österreichische Gal.

rent locations. These had to be done on the spot, in the spring and summer months, when it was possible to travel. Altar panels, oil sketches, and drawings occupied his winters at home in Vienna. On the whole his commissions came from the bishops, the lesser princes, and the smaller, more progressive monasteries of Bohemia and Hungary. His letters to the patrons, though concerned exclusively with the commissions in hand, reveal his remarkable knowledge of both religious history and classical mythology. The strong *chiaroscuro* and the powerfully drawn figures of his early style were in the Late Baroque tradition practiced in Vienna at the time of his academy training.

Maulbertsch was familiar, too, with the South German Rococo school centered on the Asam brothers and Matthäus Günther. By 1751, when he began his frescoes for the Vienna Church of the Piarists, he was using the yet lighter, more fluent manner, the yet richer, more luminous coloring characteristic of the Italian Rococo. Finally, in the last two decades of his life he adapted his style to the growing classical influence in Vienna. But although he successfully modified his forceful, often violent rhythms and distortions, his Baroque fervor of expression was too fundamental to his art to be discarded. It was this that stamped every part of his huge output with the mark of genius.

The Martyrdom of St. Jude and St. Simon, about 1760
Vienna, Österreichische Gal.

ADOLF VON MENZEL   1815-1905

The greatest realist painter of 19th-century Germany

Adolf von Menzel was born at Breslau in 1815, the eldest son of a schoolmaster. When he was 15 he helped his father, who realized his talent for drawing, to start a lithographic workshop in Berlin. This venture had been in existence for less than two years when his father died, leaving him, at 17, to support his mother and younger brothers and sisters. He therefore took commissions for lithograph letterheads, invitation cards, labels, and other hack work. Yet in his determination to become an artist he took great pains with his drawing.

Apart from a few lessons at the Berlin Academy in 1833, Menzel was almost entirely self-taught when, at the age of 19, he published lithographs of his own for the first time. These were six line drawings, illustrations for Goethe's "Künstlers Erdenwallen." They were well received, eliciting praise from the most distinguished of Berlin sculptors, Johann Gottfried Schadow. Before he was 25 Menzel had his first important commission, the illustrations for Franz Kugler's "The Life of Frederick the Great." For these, as for all his work, he made careful studies of even the tiniest details of costume and equipment. Published in Leipzig in 1840, the 400 wood engravings established his reputation even outside Germany. In France he was one of the few German artists to have a wide following. Frederick the Great

HIS WORKS INCLUDE
The Room with the Balcony, 1845
West Berlin, Staatl. Mus.
The Berlin-Potsdam Railway, 1847
West Berlin, Staatl. Mus.
Bonsoir, Messieurs, 1858
Hamburg, Kunsthalle
The Studio Wall, 1872
Hamburg, Kunsthalle
The Rolling Mill, 1875
West Berlin, Staatl. Mus.

See also pages 110, 127, 128

became his constant theme. Later print series included *The Works of Frederick the Great* and *The Army of Frederick the Great*.

Although Menzel had painted in oils from about 1837, it was not until the mid-1840's that he did really original work in this medium. Between 1845 and 1855 he painted several small works in which he reveals himself as a pioneer in Germany of open-air painting and what was to be called Impressionism. Most are family portraits (*The Artist's Sister with a Candle, Brother Arnold at the Breakfast Table, Evening Party*) or landscapes (*Building Site with Willows, The Garden of Prince Albrecht's Palace, The Berlin-Postdam Railway*). Each is the product of a direct, purely visual approach to its subject and of a fascination with the problems of light.

Today Menzel the Impressionist is generally preferred to Menzel the later painter of history. Yet he kept the greater part of these early paintings hidden

View of Salzburg
East Berlin, Staatl. Mus.

54

away in his studio, where they were seen only by his family and his most intimate friends. Toward the end of his life his attitude changed, and two years before he died *The Room with the Balcony* was purchased by the National Gallery, now part of the Staatliche Museen, West Berlin. But the general public was ignorant of this group of paintings until they caused a sensation in the retrospective Menzel Exhibition held in Berlin after his death.

Up to that moment Menzel's fame had rested on his graphic work, his history paintings and late, realistic factory pictures like *The Rolling Mill*. An oil series, *The Life and Times of Frederick the Great*, starting as early as 1849, is the best example of the grim determination, the fanatical naturalism, the meticulous, sometimes stifling detail, with which Menzel tried to force his genius into the more acceptable category of historical painting. His spontaneity as a whole was bound to suffer. Yet works like *Bonsoir, Messieurs* or *The Studio Wall* manage to recapture something of the early freshness. They also succeed with their treatment of light, particularly of artificial light.

At first even the historical paintings failed to find favor with the Prussian court at Berlin. The disturbances that came to a head in the 1848 risings in Germany had led to a sharp reaction, which could not countenance the liberal spirit of *The Life and Times of Frederick the Great*. *Bonsoir, Messieurs* was left unfinished because Menzel refused to alter the informality of the king's pose to suit the Duchess of Regensburg, who had commissioned the picture.

In 1861, however, King William I of Prussia ordered the artist to record his coronation ceremonies in a painting. Forced to obey the royal command, Menzel worked for four years on a large picture containing 132 portraits. Many honors followed: royal invitations, an honorary doctorate of Berlin University, the titles of Privy Councilor and "Excellency," the Order of the Black Eagle at 80, and a knighthood at 83. But although these successes gave Menzel pleasure, a morbid sensitivity to ridicule—he was very short—kept him always something of a recluse. He never married. Instead he was a devoted son and brother. For his sister's children he began his famous *Children's Album* in 1859, a book of charmingly painted studies of animals and other subjects. He died in Berlin in 1905, at the age of 90.

Evening Party (detail) about 1848
West Berlin, Staatl. Mus.

HANS MULTSCHER   about 1400-1467

A pioneer of realism in Late Gothic sculpture

Hans Multscher was born about 1400 at Reichenhofen in Bavaria. His years as a journeyman sculptor took him to the Netherlands and Burgundy, where he was most impressed by the monumental realism of sculptures by Claus Sluter at Dijon. By 1427 Multscher was back in southern Germany and living at Ulm, a respected citizen honored with exemption from taxes. There he remained until his death 40 years later.

Multscher's first works for the town, the figures of *Charlemagne and the Kings of Poland and Bohemia* at the town hall, contain the first signs of the sturdy, robust

HIS WORKS INCLUDE

Charlemagne and the Kings of Poland and Bohemia
Ulm, Town Hall

The Man of Sorrows, 1429
Ulm, Parish Church

The Madonna Enthroned, 1430
Munich, Bayerisches Nationalmus.

The Nativity: from the Wurzach Altarpiece, about 1437
West Berlin, Staatl. Mus.

Altarpiece, 1457-58
Sterzing, Tyrol, Parish Church

See also page 135

The Adoration of the Magi (detail):
from the Wurzach Altarpiece,
about 1437
West Berlin, Staatl. Mus.

treatment of the human body, characteristic of everything that followed from his hand. Before his time German sculptors were chiefly occupied with the elegant, linear flow of draperies. Multscher's interest was not so much in the draperies as in the form beneath, to which his *Madonna Enthroned* of 1430 bears witness.

His masterpiece, a large altarpiece with a carved shrine, was commissioned from him 26 years later for the parish church at Sterzing. The standing figures of the shrine are filled with solemn dignity and a down-to-earth bourgeois spirit new in German art. The altarpiece has folding wings painted by an artist, known as the Master of the Sterzing Altar, who may have been a member of Multscher's Ulm workshop. Multscher died in 1467.

The Madonna and Child (detail)
973-982
Essen, Cath.

See also pages 129, 130, 131

OTTONIAN MASTERPIECES   10th-11th century

Three examples of German Romanesque art

Sculpture and metalwork, like all the arts, enjoyed a second revival in late 10th-century Germany. Some of the finest pieces made for the emperors or leading churchmen survive today to attest the sensitivity and craftsmanship of Ottonian sculpture in general. Large sculptures in wood or stone and small ones in precious metals or ivory were made to adorn rood screens or to be carried in processions. Almost all held relics of saints.

Of many centers of production the Rhineland was always remarkable for its refinement. *The Gero Cross*, about 970, made for Archbishop Gero of Cologne, is the initial masterpiece of monumental Ottonian sculpture. The spirit of ancient Roman sculpture is revived in the full, heavy body of Christ. In the muscles of the right arm straining to support the downward pull of the body, in the set of the head, in the agonized yet noble features, in the hang of the loincloth, there is an expressive realism that no disregard of anatomical accuracy can dispel.

Another Rhineland product and one of the oldest German cult figures is *The Madonna and Child*, made in a Cologne workshop and donated by Abbess Matilda to her convent at Essen. A wooden core is enveloped in gold foil, so that the glistening metal and staring eyes create a strange, almost barbaric feeling, but it has, nevertheless, a vibrant tenderness.

The most important Ottonian art center was Hildesheim in Lower Saxony, whose bishop, Bernward, was a devoted patron of sculptors and architects. A famous bronze door that typifies the classical vigor of the Lower Saxon school was cast for the Church of St. Michael at Hildesheim. One wing is sculptured in relief with scenes from the book of Genesis, the other with scenes from the life of Christ. Draperies flutter and figures twist and turn as the dramatic narrative of the panels unfolds.

MICHAEL PACHER

An early Austrian master of perspective

Michael Pacher was born probably about 1435, at Neustift, in the southern Tyrol. He worked as a painter and wood carver at the neighboring town of Bruneck and at Salzburg. He was already established at Bruneck when he received his first commission, about 1461.

He visited the upper Rhine in 1470 and northern Italy probably shortly afterwards. His contemporary Mantegna was working in Padua and Mantua, and Pacher was deeply impressed by his mastery of perspective and foreshortening.

Returning to Austria, he embarked upon an altarpiece, commissioned in 1471, for the parish church of St. Wolfgang near Salzburg. Four panels of this, depicting the life of St. Wolfgang, are supposed to have been painted by Friedrich Pacher, a younger relative, perhaps his son. Michael Pacher himself embodied in this altarpiece the innovations that he had learned in Italy. A freer movement is to be seen in his still angular, Gothic figures, and space is defined and emphasized by the receding perspective lines of floor tiles, windows, columns, and vaults.

Pacher's masterpiece was the altar painting *The Fathers of the Church*, commissioned about 1483 for Neustift Church. The four fathers of the Roman Church, St. Jerome, St. Augustine, St. Gregory, and St. Ambrose, are painted in Late Gothic carved and sculptured niches. But a total effect quite unlike the Gothic of the time is produced by the exquisite detail of costume, executed in a sumptuous but somber coloring, by the psychological interpretation of the individual figures, and by the depth of shadow from which each seems to emerge. It was, in fact, Pacher's combining in this way the native Gothic tradition with essentials of Italian composition that made him an influence on German art.

In 1484 he was asked to paint a high altarpiece for the Salzburg Church of St. Francis. In 1496 he moved to Salzburg to work on it. It was unfinished when he died there two years later in 1498.

The Coronation of the Virgin, about 1475
Munich, Alte Pin.

HIS WORKS INCLUDE

Altarpiece for St. Lawrence near Bruneck, commissioned about 1461
Munich, Alte Pin.

The Flight into Egypt, about 1470
Basel, Kunstmus.

The Martyrdom of St. Thomas à Becket
Graz, Austria, Landesmus.

The Coronation of the Virgin about 1475
Munich, Alte Pin.

See also page 85

The Marriage of the Virgin (detail)
Vienna, Kunsthist. Mus.

GEORG PENCZ

Portrait of a Man with a Beard, 1543
Vienna, Kunsthist. Mus.

HIS WORKS INCLUDE

Portrait of a Man, 1531
Vienna, Österreichische Gal.

The Fall of Phaeton, 1534
Nuremberg, Germanisches Nationalmus.

Portrait of Jörg Herz, 1545
Karlsruhe, Kunsthalle

See also page 95

A follower of Dürer

Neither the place nor the date of Georg Pencz's birth is known. It is known, however, that in 1523 he obtained citizenship in Nuremberg, where he had already been for some time an assistant in Dürer's workshop. In the previous year he had helped to paint Dürer's designs (destroyed in World War II) onto the walls of the Nuremberg Town Hall. Pencz probably started as a pupil of the master, and his admiration for Dürer is evident in his work.

At the beginning of 1525 Pencz was banished from Nuremberg on charges of voicing atheistic opinions. But before the year was over he was permitted to return. Seven years later he was appointed city painter. His large illusionistic decorations were particularly in demand. In 1550 Duke Albrecht of Prussia made him his court painter, but Pencz died either in Breslau or in Leipzig on his way to take up the post.

According to Joachim von Sandrart, the first biographer of many German artists, Pencz visited Rome. He was certainly influenced by the Italian Mannerists and apparently had firsthand knowledge of Giulio Romano in particular. His ceiling, *The Fall of Phaeton*, 1534, in Nuremberg, with its massed figures and its complex foreshortenings, is modeled successfully on Giulio's illusionistic ceiling in the Palazzo del Tè in Mantua. But the effect on Pencz of his contact with Italian Mannerism was not altogether a happy one. A hard, smooth texture characterizes some of his later work.

No such criticism is attached to his portraits, however, which are indebted successively to Dürer, to Giorgione and Titian (for a freer handling), and finally, during the 1540's, to the restrained Mannerism of Bronzino. Thus it is on his portraits that Pencz's reputation largely depends, though his small engravings are also noteworthy. Of these, the copperplate engravings are signed from about 1522 to 1530 with the monogram I. B. (Iorg Bentz) and after 1531 with a G. P. The earlier group shows figures from the Old Testament side by side with allegorical characters.

HIS WORKS INCLUDE

St. Michael and Lucifer, 1606
Augsburg, Armory

Fountain of Neptune
Danzig (Gdansk), Langer Markt

See also page 140

HANS REICHLE

A pioneer of Baroque sculpture in Germany

Hans Reichle was born about 1570 in Schongau into a family of sculptors. He probably had his first art lessons in his father's workshop. But it was in Italy, under the famous Florentine sculptor Giovanni da Bologna, that he perfected his technique. To the polished Mannerism learned from his master, Reichle added a new, Baroque sense of drama.

Back in Bavaria at the age of 25, he worked in Munich on a large kneeling figure of *St. Mary Magdalen* that was to be added to a crucifix by Giovanni da

Bologna. This crucifix was in the possession of King William IV of Bavaria, who wished the completed group to form part of an elaborate monument to his family. This project was never realized.

In 1596 Reichle was called to Brixen in the Tyrol, to begin what proved to be a long and fruitful association with the court of the prince bishop. Here he spent the greater part of six years on a series of terracotta statues of members of the Hapsburg family. On the death of the prince bishop in 1602, his more economical successor broke off the work and dismissed Reichle with honors. The sculptor returned to Florence, the scene of his earlier studies.

In 1603, however, he was invited to Augsburg in connection with a bronze statue of St. Michael, which was to adorn the newly built Augsburg Armory. Reichle's St. Michael, holding aloft his flaming sword and charged with irresistible force, towers above the agonized figure of the conquered devil, whose face is the embodiment of impotent evil. It was this group, a major achievement of the early German Baroque, that confirmed Reichle's reputation.

In 1607, Reichle returned to Brixen and, as commissions for sculpture were still few, practiced mainly as an architect. By 1611 he had attained a permanent salaried position under the prince bishop. His patron died in 1613, but after four years and a short visit to Venice, Reichle was reconfirmed in his court office and enabled to remain in Brixen until his death in 1642. The only important commission that he executed away from Brixen in these years, his bronze Neptune fountain at Danzig (now Gdansk) on the Baltic, is in a soft, rich, decorative style unusual to Reichle, the result of his stay in Venice.

St. Michael and Lucifer, 1606
Augsburg, Armory

ALFRED RETHEL   1816-1859

A gifted but constantly frustrated draftsman and painter

Alfred Rethel was born and reared on his father's estate at Diepenbend near Aachen. His talent for drawing was obvious at an early age. About 100 sheets of drawings done before he was 13, early proof of his taste for battles and heroic themes, are now in the Aachen Museum. At 13 Rethel went to the Düsseldorf Academy, where he remained for seven years and absorbed, under Wilhelm von Schadow, an academic interpretation of late Romanticism. From 1836 to 1847, apart from a year in Italy, he lived in Frankfurt.

In 1839, invited to take part in the competition for a contract to decorate a room in the town hall at Aachen with fresco scenes from the life of Charlemagne, Rethel produced designs of such originality that the other competitors withdrew. The contract was his, but before he could embark upon it he had to wait seven years while a long and violent altercation was carried on. The main question in dispute was whether or not the south windows of the room should be blocked in so as to allow more space for the frescoes. Rethel finally appealed to the king, who ruled in 1847 that they should.

Although the Aachen frescoes are outstanding examples of German history

Sketch for a Monument to Gutenberg (detail)
Frankfurt-am-Main, Städelsches Kunstinst.

Bridal Procession in Spring (detail)
about 1847
Dresden, Gemäldegal.

painting of the time, they gave Rethel himself little satisfaction. By 1852 only four out of an agreed eight were finished. The rest had to be painted from Rethel's cartoons by his pupil Josef Kehren. Rethel's mind was too disturbed for him to continue the work himself.

Private as well as professional stresses, including the long illness of his wife, had something to do with the situation. Rethel spent his last six years, insane and helpless, in the care of his mother and sister. He died at Düsseldorf in 1859.

Like so many contemporary German artists, Rethel was by nature a draftsman rather than a painter. He left comparatively few paintings, frescoes, and oils on religious and historical subjects and even these are markedly linear in design. The events, however, as in the woodcut series *This, Too, Is a Dance of Death*, 1848, were sometimes contemporary ones. This series and two other woodcuts occupied with the figure of Death, *Death as a Ruthless Reaper*, 1847, and *Death as a Friend*, 1851, are the works by which Rethel is chiefly remembered.

LUDWIG ADRIAN RICHTER 1803-1884

A painter, draftsman, and illustrator of home life and fairy tales

Ludwig Adrian Richter was born the son of a copper engraver in Dresden in 1803. From the age of 12 he worked with his father, an apprenticeship that in his own view "consisted only of work and I learned nothing, or only very little." The little, however, a thorough grounding in his father's craft, later stood him in excellent stead when he turned to book illustration.

Meanwhile, as a boy of 17, Richter accompanied the Russian prince Narishkin to France as a landscape draftsman. The prince treated him badly, and Richter profited little from the trip. Three years later a traveling scholarship from a Dresden publisher enabled him to go, by way of Austria, where the Salzburg scenery impressed him, to Rome. He fell under the spell of Joseph Anton Koch, an Austrian mountain painter domiciled there. Richter's first landscape painting, *The Watzmann*, 1824, is derived almost in its entirety from Koch's *Schmadribach Fall*, painted two years earlier. Koch's influence dominated his work for some years to come. In 1835, however, a visit to the upper Elbe valley awoke an interest in his native landscape and caused him to discard the Italianate style in favor of a simpler, more sincere manner.

Richter had been appointed drawing master at the Meissen porcelain factory in 1826. There he remained until he succeeded ten years later to his father's position as professor at the Dresden Academy. At the same time his fruitful association with the Leipzig publisher Georg Wigand began. Wigand was preparing a series of ten volumes of woodcut illustrations under the title "Picturesque and Romantic Germany," and Richter was invited to participate. His drawings proved so successful, despite the poor quality of the woodcut prints made from them, that four of the ten volumes were devoted to them.

Happiest among his family or with friends, Richter was at his best in the portrayal of homely, intimate scenes from the life around him: the little man and his family, peasants at home or in the countryside, children and young people, fairy-tale characters. He saw all these with a serene, benevolent, and observant eye and reproduced their freshness through his mastery of technique.

TILMAN RIEMENSCHNEIDER   about 1460-1531

A sensitive sculptor who helped the transition from Gothic to Renaissance in Germany

Tilman Riemenschneider was born about 1460, the son of a Heiligenstadt copper-smith. In 1465 his father and uncle were involved in a quarrel waging between the abbey community of St. Martin and the Heiligenstadt Council, and they were forced to leave the city. Riemenschneider spent his childhood in Österode, not far from Heiligenstadt, while his uncle settled in Würzburg, attained eminent status in the church and gave his brother unstinted advice and help. It was probably the connection with his uncle that took the young Tilman, newly trained as a sculptor, to Würzburg. There he lived from 1483 until his death in 1531, marrying four times and rising to a position of distinction as artist, citizen, and even mayor of Würzburg. His civic career was cut short, however, when he was thrown into prison, tortured, and heavily fined for sympathizing with the peasant revolt of 1525. He spent his last few years, a broken man, living in poverty and isolation.

Riemenschneider's first big sculpture commission, the altarpiece of *The Life of St. Mary Magdalen*, 1490, was executed in the perfect craftmanship of the Late Gothic

HIS WORKS INCLUDE

Altarpiece of the Life of St. Mary Magdalen, 1490
Münnerstadt, Parish Church
West Berlin, Staatl. Mus.
Munich, Alte Pin.

Tombs of Henry II and his Wife Kunigunde, 1499-1513
Bamberg, Cath.

Tomb of Konrad of Schaumburg, about 1500
Würzburg, Cath.

See also page 136

Kneeling Angel, early 16th century
London, V. and A.

The Evangelist Luke
West Berlin, Staatl. Mus.

St. Valentine, about 1500
East Berlin, Staatl. Mus.

61

in which he persevered to the end. Here it embraces the minutest details of finger and toenails. But rather than cover his carving with the polychrome painting and gilding customary at the time, Riemenschneider was the first to leave the natural texture of the wood unadorned. This innovation had no immediate popular appeal. In 1504 the Nuremberg sculptor Veit Stoss was commissioned to paint and gild the altarpiece.

During the first quarter of the 16th century Riemenschneider presided over a large and productive workshop. In addition to altarpieces and tombs in both wood and stone, he undertook a number of single figures of which the last ones, in the new spirit of the Renaissance, are full of a mature, observant sense of form and insight into human emotions.

PHILIPP OTTO RUNGE 1777-1810

A Romantic painter of portraits and allegories

Philipp Otto Runge was born in 1777 in Wolgast, at that time part of Swedish Pomerania. It was not until he was 20 that he began to take drawing lessons. From 1799 he studied for two years each at the Copenhagen and Dresden Academies. In 1803 he settled in Hamburg with his wife and children.

In 1801 Runge visited the greatest German Romantic landscape painter, Caspar Friedrich, at his home town of Greifswald. His own religious feeling and his interest in Romantic poetry were supplemented by his reading of the 17th-century mystic Jakob Böhme.

Amarylis Formosissima (detail) 1808
Hamburg, Kunsthalle

Self-portrait in a Blue Coat, 1805
Hamburg, Kunsthalle

Morning: from The Four Phases of the Day, 1809 *Hamburg, Kunsthalle*

Runge set himself to paint a cycle of cosmic allegories, *The Four Phases of the Day*. The four phases were to be morning, day, evening, and night. Although Runge worked on the cycle for the latter part of his short life, he never completed the final versions, which he envisaged as large murals in some sacred building.

As well as sacred compositions and works of imagination, he painted excellent portraits, of his family, relations and friends. One of the best of these, the portrait group of his parents with his two children, is a moving presentation of the contrast between the old and the young. The old people are curiously similar to each other, their somewhat harsh features expressive of the heavy apathy of old age; the small children are absorbed in their own primitive world.

Runge used light to emphasize the expressiveness of some of his portraits. In his self-portrait, touches of light on face, neck, ruffle, and hand heighten the sensitivity and romanticism of the dreamy, brooding face. Color was also a problem that never ceased to fascinate him.

Runge wore himself out with his ceaseless efforts to capture in paint his sense of the infinite. When he died in Hamburg in 1810, at the age of 33, he left much of his work unfinished.

HIS WORKS INCLUDE

Self-portrait, 1802
Hamburg, Kunsthalle

Portrait of Daniel Runge, 1804
Hamburg, Kunsthalle

See also page 106

JOACHIM VON SANDRART   1606-1686

A widely traveled painter and writer on art

Joachim von Sandrart was born in 1606 at Speyer, on the Rhine. He received a sound education, first in Nuremberg, and then in Prague as a pupil of the engraver Egidius Sadeler. Afterwards he proceeded to France and Holland, where he studied under the painter Gerard van Honthorst, the foremost Dutch follower of Caravaggio. In 1627 master and pupil went together to London.

After two years there, Sandrart set out for Italy. He spent six years in Rome, counting the most eminent artists and scholars among his friends. He found a patron in the Marchese Giustiniani and helped to spread the knowledge of antiquity with his huge volume of engravings of the Giustiniani collection of classical statues.

When Sandrart left Italy in 1635, he went first to Frankfurt and then, in order to avoid the threatening religious wars, to Amsterdam in 1642. Through his wife he acquired a fine estate in Stockau, to which he returned after 1645 to live the life of a country gentleman for 15 years.

Sandrart's religious, historical, and narrative paintings are Italianate in manner, whereas his portraits, which include some of his finest work, reveal a Netherlandish influence. This is especially true of his two great portrait groups, *The Company of Captain Bicker*, 1638, and the imposing *Ambassador's Banquet* painted in 1649 for the Nuremberg Town Hall. His complicated style exactly suited the taste of his patrons. In 1653 he was raised to the nobility.

His distinguished career was the result of his genius as a collector, connoisseur,

Self-portrait:
from The Ambassador's Banquet, 1649
Nuremberg, Städtische Kunstsamm.

HIS WORKS INCLUDE

Portrait of Johann Maximilian zum Jungen, 1636
Frankfurt-am-Main, Historisches Mus.

The Company of Captain Bicker, 1638
Amsterdam, Rijksmus.

The Ambassador's Banquet, 1649
Nuremberg, Städtische Kunstsamm.

See also page 100

and man of letters, as well as his excellence as a painter and draftsman. He is best known today for his book "The German Academy," 1675, a collection of artists' biographies combined with a treatise on painting.

In 1660 Sandrart sold his Stockau estate and went to live in Augsburg. In 1674 he married for the second time and moved to Nuremberg, where he died in 1686.

J. Sandrart

JOHANN GOTTFRIED SCHADOW 1764-1860

A sculptor who introduced realism into a classical vogue

Self-portrait, about 1790
East Berlin, Staatl. Mus.

Johann Gottfried Schadow was born in Berlin in 1764. His first teacher was the Fleming Jan Pieter Anton Tassaert, a Baroque sculptor at the Prussian court of Berlin. Then at 21 Schadow eloped to Italy with a Viennese girl and spent two years studying in Rome. There he met Antonio Canova, already famous at 28 as the strictest classicist among living sculptors. On his return to Berlin in 1787, Schadow found a patron in von Heinitz, curator of the Berlin Academy, who next year obtained for him the position of court sculptor left vacant by the death of Tassaert.

Schadow's concept of sculpture was very different from the Baroque of Tassaert, and without the implications of pathos or sentiment that marked the Neoclassicism of Canova. The classic form of Schadow's sepulcher of Count Alexander von der Mark, 1787-91, for example, is firmly based on reality and is in striking contrast to the somewhat pompous artificiality of German art at that time. The simplicity and the directness of much of his early work did not please King Friedrich Wilhelm III, who was more inclined to favor a young sculptor, Christian Rauch. Schadow's charming marble group of the two crown princesses Luise and Friederike of Prussia, 1795, long stood almost unknown in a guest room of the Berlin palace. His

Charity
Antwerp, Mus. Royal des B-A.

Cupid Asleep (detail) 1798
Marburg, Universitätsmus.

64

monument to Fieldmarshal Blücher, 1819, for the city of Rostock is a stern and sober work in a very "Prussian" spirit, despite the lionskin that the poet Goethe persuaded him to add.

Although Friedrich Wilhelm's successor, Friedrich Wilhelm IV, appreciated Schadow's talent and loaded him with honors, Schadow seemed to set little store by such distinctions, living quietly in Berlin until his death in 1860 at the age of 96.

Schadow himself made an important contribution to the development of German sculpture, despite the indifference of the Prussian court. Without him the Berlin School would hardly have won recognition in the rest of Europe.

HIS WORKS INCLUDE

Sepulcher of Count Alexander von der Mark, 1787-91
West Berlin, Staatl. Mus.

Monument to Frederick the Great, about 1793
Stettin, Poland

Monument to General Joachim Ziethen, about 1794
East Berlin, Staatl. Mus.

Monument to Fieldmarshal Blücher, 1819
Rostock

See also page 144

ANDREAS SCHLÜTER   about 1660/64-1714

A powerful Baroque sculptor and architect

Warrior's Mask, about 1697
East Berlin, Mus. für Deutsche Geschichte

Andreas Schlüter was born about 1660/64 in Hamburg and educated as a sculptor at Danzig (now Gdansk) on the Baltic. After traveling to France and Italy, he went to Warsaw in 1689 as a sculptor in the service of the king of Poland, John Sobieski. Five years later he was called to Berlin by the elector, Friedrich III, afterwards King Frederick I of Prussia.

One of Schlüter's first official responsibilities in Berlin was a bronze monument of his patron, cast in 1697. He was engaged about the same time on the decoration of the Berlin Armory. Here his fine sculptured masks of dying soldiers, his Medusa heads, and his groups of trophies and helmets demonstrate his peculiar talent for adapting decorative sculpture to its architectural setting.

His best-known statue, however, is the magnificent equestrian monument to *The Elector of Brandenburg*, father of Friedrich III. The pedestal reliefs, though designed by Schlüter, were carried out a little later by his pupils. The monument is the most impressive of its kind in Germany. In style it owes a great deal to Italian, French, and even ancient Roman models. At the same time Schlüter's interpretation of the subject, mirroring the pride and confidence of the rider in the prancing movement of his horse, was his own.

Schlüter was now at the height of his fame. He was in sole charge of the building program for the new Berlin palace. In addition to this enormous task, he directed the Berlin Academy and undertook further commissions that included the ornate sarcophagi of King Frederick, Queen Charlotte, and their son, Friedrich Ludwig.

Schlüter's association with the Prussian court ended in disaster when a huge mint tower that he was building in the palace grounds collapsed. His jealous colleagues were quick to take advantage, so that he eventually had to abandon architecture altogether. In the execution of a few private sculpture commissions that remained to him he adopted a new, lighter, more fluid handling. In 1714 he was called to Russia, to the court of Peter the Great at St. Petersburg (now Leningrad). But Schlüter was already a sick man, and died there the same year.

HIS WORKS INCLUDE

East Pediment
Warsaw, Krasinsky Palace

Tomb of Count Goldsmith Männlich, 1700
Berlin, St. Nikolaus

Pulpit, 1703
Berlin, St. Maria

Tombs of King Frederick I of Prussia, Queen Charlotte, and their son Friedrich Ludwig, 1705 *et seq.*
Berlin, Cath.

Reliefs
Berlin, Kamecke House

See also page 141

Frau Bianca von Quandt, *1820*
East Berlin, Staatl. Mus.

HIS WORKS INCLUDE

The Marriage at Cana, about 1818
Hamburg, Kunsthalle

Frescoes
Rome, Casa Massimo, Ariosto Room

Frescoes of the Nibelungen Saga
Munich, Residenz

See also page 108

JULIUS SCHNORR VON CAROLSFELD 1794-1872

A Nazarene painter and draftsman

Julius Schnorr von Carolsfeld was born in Leipzig in 1794, the son of a painter. At 17 he went to study at the Vienna Academy. But the classicism taught there attracted him less than the landscapes of Joseph Anton Koch or the work of his friend Ferdinand Olivier. Olivier was the most talented landscapist in the Nazarene brotherhood, whose aim was to rejuvenate German painting by reviving Christian art in the spirit of late medieval Germany combined with that of 15th-century Italy.

In 1817 Schnorr made his first journey to Italy. In 1818 he was in close contact with some Nazarenes who had already made their home in Rome. The group ideal was to cover large walls with murals. Schnorr achieved this goal when the Marchese Carlo Massimo commissioned the brotherhood to decorate three rooms in his Roman villa.

In 1825 King Ludwig I of Bavaria summoned him to Munich to paint scenes from Homer's "Odyssey" on the walls of the royal palace. Schnorr accordingly spent the year 1826 in Sicily making landscape studies with this subject in view. But the king had changed his mind in the meantime. He now wished the saga of the Nibelungen to be the theme of his frescoes, and it was thus that five rooms were painted. Another royal commission followed, again for the Munich palace, where three rooms of the banqueting house were to be decorated with episodes from the history of the reigns of Charlemagne, Barbarossa, and Rudolph of Hapsburg. The actual painting was carried out from Schnorr's designs by his pupils. His best period was already past. His later work lacked the earlier spontaneity and genuine feeling, so that his huge idealized historical scenes appear cold and empty.

In 1846 Schnorr was invited to take up appointments as director of the Dresden Gallery and professor at the academy. There he died 26 years later, in 1872.

K. Andrews The Nazarenes Oxford, 1964

HIS WORKS INCLUDE

PAINTINGS

Madonna and Child in an Interior
Basel, Kunstmus.

Madonna in the Rose Bower, 1473
Colmar, France, Monastery of St. Martin

ENGRAVINGS

The Carrying of the Cross

St. Sebastian

The Madonna and Child in the
Enclosed Garden

See also page 115

MARTIN SCHONGAUER probably about 1430/35-1491

A painter and engraver of Alsace

The date of Martin Schongauer's birth at Colmar in Alsace can be deduced from a portrait of him, as a young man of about 20, that bears the date 1453. This was painted by the Master of the Legend of St. Ulrich and later retouched by Hans Burgkmair.

He was the son of goldsmith, Caspar Schongauer, who had his workshop at Colmar. Martin's elder brothers followed their father's trade, while he himself was apparently intended for the church. However, he was apprenticed with a local master and then visited the Netherlands and Burgundy, in the course of long travels as a journeyman artist. He became familiar with Flemish painting, especially that of Roger van der Weyden, of whose *Last Judgment*, about 1446, he made a copy. He also went to Spain, where he made nine drawings of heads of Spanish Moors, some of which were later used in his engravings. In 1471 he settled again at Colmar.

Although Schongauer was highly respected as a painter, only a few paintings can be said with any certainty to be his. Apart from the impressive, over life-size *Madonna in the Rose Bower* of 1473, most of these are small. There is an early and tentative *Madonna and Child in an Interior*, with traces of the Netherlandish influence that was to dominate Schongauer's mature work, such as his little panels of *The Holy Family* and *The Nativity*. Fragments of a wall painting of *The Last Judgment* have recently been uncovered in the Church of St. Stephen at Breisach. Schongauer moved to Breisach in 1488 and died there three years later.

About 115 engravings remain with his signature. Although reminiscent of Master E. S., they contain a personal, powerful treatment of space and a decorative richness of line, qualities that may be the result of Schongauer's early experience of the goldsmith's shop. These prints play a significant part in the development of German engraving, particularly in the impression they were to make on the young Dürer, who came to Colmar to visit the master.

Monk Drinking
Washington, D. C., N. G.

KONRAD VON SOEST
active about 1400-after 1420

An early master of the Soft Style

Konrad von Soest was born probably in Dortmund, Westphalia, about 25 miles west of Soest, the place of origin of his family. He lived, worked, and married at Dortmund.

Konrad von Soest is one of the earliest painters in the whole of Germany to whom a number of works or workshop productions can be attributed with any certainty. A "painter Konrad," at the height of his reputation, is mentioned between 1413 and 1422 in the chronicles of the brotherhood attached to the Dortmund Church of St. Nicholas, for which he doubtless worked. Only two altarpieces signed by him survive today. The earlier contains 13 panels of the life of Christ and bears an indistinct date, probably 1403.

Although it is not certain that Master Konrad actually traveled in France and the Burgundian territories, there is no doubt that he was familiar with Franco-Burgundian art. By about 1400, like Master Francke a year or two later, he clearly had some firsthand knowledge of French manuscript illuminations. Nevertheless, his style was largely a product of the native Westphalian tradition, with all the charming characteristics of the peculiarly German form of International Gothic called the Soft Style. This was to dominate German painting during the first half of the 15th century.

The Crucifixion (detail) 1403
Bad Wildungen, Parish Church

See also page 79

VEIT STOSS

about 1445-1533

A Gothic and northern Renaissance sculptor of force and individuality

Veit Stoss was born about 1445 in Horb in Swabia. In 1476 he was already a master sculptor of wide repute in Nuremberg, but he settled at Cracow in Poland to execute a commission from the German community there, which wished to improve its church with a large carved altarpiece of the Virgin Mary. Finished in 1487, it proved to be one of the great works of art of its time, and is the largest German carved altarpiece extant (40 feet high, 33 feet wide). Stoss stayed in Cracow for 19 years in all, esteemed both as citizen and artist by Germans and Poles alike. His privileges included exemption from taxes and among his patrons was the king of Poland.

Stoss' harshly realistic human figures, his draperies bunched up and falling in long, angular folds, were in the German Gothic tradition but, for sheer forcefulness, far in excess of anything previously achieved.

In 1496 Stoss returned to Nuremberg, and devoted himself to the adornment of the Nuremberg churches with figures and reliefs in wood and stone. As he followed the Late Gothic custom of painting and gilding his wooden products, he was asked, in 1504, to supervise the polychroming of *The St. Mary Magdalen Altarpiece*, 1490, of his Würzburg contemporary, Tilman Riemenschneider. The latter, more originally but less acceptably, had preferred to let his unadorned wooden surfaces speak for themselves. Stoss undertook at the same time to paint four folding wings for the same altarpiece with scenes from the life of St. Kilian. These are his only paintings known today, though several excellent engravings by him survive.

In 1503 Stoss was prosecuted for fraud by the Nuremberg City Council, and, although he escaped the death penalty, he was heavily fined, imprisoned, branded, and forbidden to leave Nuremberg without the consent of the authorities. This injunction ran counter to his restless temperament and he constantly disobeyed it, so that the rest of his life was spent in fruitless lawsuits. His good name being firmly established outside Nuremberg despite his poor reputation within the city, he appealed for support directly to Emperor Maximilian. The emperor gave him a letter of rehabilitation and permission to leave Nuremberg, which the councilors refused to recognize. Thus the quarrel was resolved only by the death of Stoss in 1533, an embittered old man with nothing remaining to him of the fortune he had amassed.

The Virgin and Child, 1500-10
London, V. and A.

HIS WORKS INCLUDE

Altarpiece of the Virgin, 1477-87
Cracow, Poland, St. Mary's

Tomb of King Casimir IV Jagello
of Poland, 1492
Cracow, Poland, Cath.

The Virgin and Child, 1500-10
London, V. and A.

The Crucifixion, 1510
Nuremberg, Germanisches Nationalmus.

Altarpiece, 1520-23
Bamberg, Cath.

See also page 138

JOHANN HEINRICH WILHELM TISCHBEIN

1751-1829

A painter and engraver known as "Goethe" Tischbein

Johann Heinrich Wilhelm Tischbein was born in 1751 in Haida, Hesse, into a large family that had produced painters for three generations before him. Tischbein went to stay with an art dealer cousin in Hamburg, and restored and copied all kinds of old master paintings. Not surprisingly, he developed an eclectic style.

After visiting Amsterdam in 1771, Tischbein lived first at Bremen and then at the court of Berlin, where he received many portrait commissions. To this day his reputation rests largely on his portraits, which, in fact, he disliked to paint.

The new Kassel Academy offered him a stipend on which to travel to Italy, and he saw Venice, Florence, and finally Rome, where he looked at the works of Raphael and Michelangelo and painted landscapes. On his way back to Germany in 1781, he stopped for a year in Zurich. There he was entertained by the philosopher Lavater.

Tischbein was living in Kassel when Goethe, a stranger to him but interested in his painting, spoke on his behalf with Archduke Ernst of Gotha. As a result, funds were forthcoming for a second visit to Italy in 1783. There in 1786 Tischbein first met Goethe. His large *Portrait of Goethe in the Campagna*, which gave him the nickname "Goethe" Tischbein, was painted in the following year. He traveled with Goethe to Naples, where he eventually settled and became director of the Naples Academy. After 16 years in Italy, Tischbein returned in 1799 to Kassel. He married, and died at Eutin in 1829.

Tischbein's great interest was history painting. His long and diversified career and his susceptibility to new influences carried his art through various styles. He worked at first in the Rococo tradition of his uncle and from about 1780 in a more classical manner. This in turn was considerably modified during his last phase by the rising German Romanticism.

Portrait of the Artist and his Brother Jacob (detail) 1782
Frankfurt-am-Main, Goethehaus

Interior of a Kitchen (detail)
Hamburg, Kunsthalle

HIS WORKS INCLUDE

Winter Landscape, 1781
Oldenburg, Landesmus.

Konradin of Hohenstaufen and Friedrich of Austria Playing a Boardgame in Prison, about 1782
Gotha, Schlossmus.

Portrait of Goethe in the Campagna 1787
Frankfurt-am-Main, Städelsches Kunstinst.

Hector's Farewell, 1812
Oldenburg, Landesmus.

See also page 104

PAUL TROGER   1698-1762

An Austrian painter of Baroque illusionism

Paul Troger was born in 1698 at Welsberg in the Austrian Tyrol. He was taken as a boy into the household of the counts of Firmian, where his artistic talent was recognized and carefully fostered. Later the Firmian family obtained a grant for him from the archbishop of Gurk, enabling him to continue his training in Italy.

HIS WORKS INCLUDE

Altar panel, 1722
Kaltern, Tyrol, Heiligenkreuz Chapel

Frescoes, about 1731
Melk, Austria, Stiftsbibl.

Frescoes, 1748-50
Brixen, Tyrol, Cath.

See also page 101

St. Andrew, about 1740
Vienna, Österreichische Gal.

This first Italian visit was spent mostly in Venice, whose exponents of Baroque art made a profound impression on Troger. His first important work, an altar panel for Heiligenkreuz Chapel at Kaltern, was painted in 1722 on his return to the Tyrol. When he went back to Italy he stayed this time for three years.

In Rome he studied ancient art as well as recent masters. The illusionism of Andrea Pozzo particularly fascinated him; after his return to Austria he achieved similar effects in the dome of St. Cajetan in Salzburg, which he frescoed in 1728 for his patron, the archbishop of Gurk.

Soon afterwards Troger moved to Vienna, found a new patron in Count Gundacker von Althan, obtained the title of court painter, and joined the Vienna Academy.

In 1751 he was given a professorship at the academy and three years later he became its director. His effective teaching had considerable influence upon the tastes of a younger generation of artists in Vienna. He died in Vienna in 1762.

Troger was fortunate in living at a time when Austria possessed wealthy, enlightened patrons and a belief in painting as the most important form of decoration. Throughout his life he had plentiful commissions. He spent the summer months in lower Austria, Moravia, or Hungary, frescoing numerous walls, domes, and ceilings. In the winter he painted numbers of altar panels and other subjects in Vienna.

The rather clumsy composition and gaudy coloring of Troger's early style gave way in Vienna to a lighter, more elegant touch. These in turn led to the visionary dynamism of his frescoes of 1733 at Altenburg. Of works in his later, mature style the best examples are the magnificent fresco decorations, 1748-50, in Brixen Cathedral, for which he originally proposed two alternative plans; the frescoes were to be framed either in plasterwork, or in the painted illusion of plasterwork and of architecture—a much more elaborate, painstaking, and expensive setting. It was characteristic of the period that the second project was adopted. The finished work transcends the Baroque style, to display all the decorative qualities of Rococo.

Altarpiece from Soest (detail)
about 1250-70
West Berlin, Staatl. Mus.

WESTPHALIA, ALTARPIECE FROM SOEST   about 1250-70

An early panel painting

Westphalia had flourishing centers of Romanesque art. The three earliest panel paintings in Germany come from churches in Soest.

Wooden panels, for example, the sides of cupboards and chests, were painted throughout the Middle Ages, but practically none is known until the end of the 12th century, when the earliest of the three Soest altar paintings was made. A single panel containing three sections, it was an altar retable, a type that was later largely superseded by bigger altarpieces with folding wings.

The later Soest panels are of the same triple, unjointed type. But the second, the product of the early 13th century, already has more lively figures; while the third, painted in the late Romanesque style about 1250-70, and executed with an extraordinary agitation of line, entirely abandons the quieter manner of the first two retables. The mighty figure of the Father in the central paintings seems charged with an inner tension that spreads to the restless, jagged draperies and the architecture of His throne.

See also page 75

KONRAD WITZ 1400/10-1444/45

A painter of a revolutionary realism

Konrad Witz was born at Rottweil in southern Germany between 1400 and 1410. As a young man he spent some time in the Netherlands; later, he settled in Switzerland. In 1434 he was permitted to enter the Basel painters' guild. He married the niece of a busy German painter, with whom he collaborated on murals (about 1441, now lost) for the city armory. By 1445 he was dead. In the ten brief years of his working life in Basel and Geneva, Witz produced all his paintings. Yet they suffice to establish him as one of the great artists of his time.

Witz's training left him fully conversant with the means by which the van Eycks and the Master of Flémalle had injected new life into the art of the Netherlands. He shared their love of materials, rich brocades, folds of heavy drapery, polished metal surfaces, and their fondness for portraiture. The features of King David in *The Redemption Altarpiece* of 1435, for example, are those of Emperor Sigismund.

But there was more to Witz than merely a debt to the Flemings. In the background of his panel of St. Catherine and St. Mary Magdalen is the view of a street; one house with two painted, carved figures in its groundfloor shopwindow was probably Witz's own. He may have been a woodcarver as well as a painter, having a feeling for the grand and the monumental, as the same panel shows.

One of his last works, *Christ Walking on the Water*, 1444, a panel of an altarpiece commissioned by the bishop of Geneva, sets a particular scene. The shadows are those of mid-afternoon on a summer day, the place is very clearly Lake Geneva, with Mont Blanc seen from Les Paques. This is the earliest known presentation of a recognizable view.

HIS WORKS INCLUDE
Altarpiece of the Redemption, 1435
Basel, Kunstmus.
St. Catherine and St. Mary Magdalen
Strasbourg, Mus. des B-A.
Christ Walking on the Water, 1444
Geneva, Mus. d'Art et d'Histoire
The Annunciation, about 1445
Nuremberg, Germanisches Nationalmus.

See also page 84

The Deliverance of St. Peter
(detail) 1444
Geneva, Mus. d'Art et d'Histoire

Christ Walking on the Water (detail) 1444
Geneva, Mus. d'Art et d'Histoire

MANUSCRIPT: REICHENAU (Lake Constance)
The Annunciation to the Shepherds: page of The Pericope Book of Henry II,
about 1007-12 *vellum* *11 × 8¼ in.*
Munich, Bayerische Staatsbibliothek

MANUSCRIPT: COLOGNE St. Pantaleon: page of a Book of Gospels (detail)
about 1170 *vellum* *approximately actual size*
Cologne, Stadtarchiv

WESTPHALIA Altarpiece from Soest, about 1250-70
tempera on panel 25 × 47 in.
West Berlin, Staatliche Museen

COLOGNE The Crucifixion: center panel of an altarpiece, about 1320
tempera on panel 21¼ × 16¼ *in.*
Cologne, Wallraf-Richartz-Museum

MASTER BERTRAM God Creating the Animals: panel from the Grabow Altar, 1379
tempera on panel $33\frac{7}{8} \times 22\frac{1}{2}$ in.
Hamburg, Kunsthalle

BOHEMIA   The Madonna and Child from Glatz, about 1350
tempera on panel   73¼ × 37⅞ in.
West Berlin, Staatliche Museen

KONRAD VON SOEST   The Crucifixion: center panel of an altarpiece, 1403
tempera on panel   62⅝ × 62⅝ in.
Bad Wildungen, Parish Church

MASTER OF ST. VERONICA The Madonna and Child with a Pea Blossom, about 1400
tempera on panel   21¼ × 14⅛ in.
Nuremberg, Germanisches Nationalmuseum

MASTER FRANCKE   The Mocking of St. Thomas of Canterbury: altarpiece panel, after 1424

tempera on panel   39 × 35⅜ in.
Hamburg, Kunsthalle

MASTER OF THE UPPER RHINE The Garden of Paradise, about 1410 *tempera on panel 10¾ × 13¼ in.*
Frankfurt-am-Main, Historisches Museum

STEFAN LOCHNER The Presentation in the Temple, 1447 *tempera on panel* 54¾ × 49⅝ *in.*
Darmstadt, Hessisches Landesmuseum

KONRAD WITZ Joachim and Anna at the Golden Gate: altarpiece panel, about 1440
tempera on panel   61$\frac{3}{8}$ × 47$\frac{5}{8}$ in.
Basel, Kunstmuseum

MICHAEL PACHER St. Wolfgang Forces the Devil to Hold the Prayerbook for him: altarpiece panel, about 1483
oil on panel $40\frac{1}{4} \times 35\frac{7}{8}$ *in.*
Munich, Alte Pinakothek

MASTER OF THE ST. BARTHOLOMEW ALTARPIECE   The Crucifixion: center panel
of an altarpiece, about 1500   *tempera on panel*   *42⅛ × 31¼ in.*
Cologne, Wallraf-Richartz-Museum

LUCAS CRANACH the **ELDER** The Rest on the Flight into Egypt, 1504
oil on panel   27⅛ × 20⅛ in.
West Berlin, Staatliche Museen

ALBRECHT DÜRER Self-portrait in a Fur Coat, 1500 *oil on panel 26¼ × 19¼ in.*
Munich, Alte Pinakothek

ALBRECHT DÜRER   The Four Apostles 1526   *oil on panel* $84\frac{3}{4} \times 29\frac{7}{8}$ *in. each*
Munich, Alte Pinakothek

HANS BURGKMAIR   St. John on Patmos: center panel of an altarpiece, 1518
oil on panel   60¼ × 49⅜ in.
Munich, Alte Pinakothek

MATHIS GOTHARDT, called GRÜNEWALD The Crucifixion: altarpiece panel, about 1524
oil on panel 77⅞ × 59⅞ in.
Karlsruhe, Kunsthalle

ALBRECHT ALTDORFER   Worth Castle and the Scheuchenberg, about 1527
parchment on panel $11\frac{7}{8} \times 8\frac{5}{8}$ in.
Munich, Alte Pinakothek

HANS BALDUNG, called GRIEN Two Witches, 1523 *oil on panel 25⅝ × 17¾ in.*
Frankfurt-am-Main, Städelsches Kunstinstitut

HANS HOLBEIN the YOUNGER   Portrait of Georg Gisze, 1532   *oil on panel*   37¾×33⅛ *in.*
West Berlin, Staatliche Museen

GEORG PENCZ Portrait of Jörg Herz, 1545 *oil on canvas $42\frac{7}{8} \times 38\frac{5}{8}$ in.*
Karlsruhe, Kunsthalle

HANS VON AACHEN The Victory of Truth, 1598 *oil on copper* *22 × 18½ in.*
Munich, Alte Pinakothek

96

GEORG FLEGEL   Larder Lit by a Candle, about 1630-35   *oil on canvas* $28\frac{1}{4} \times 23\frac{5}{8}$ *in.*
Karlsruhe, Kunsthalle

ADAM ELSHEIMER   Morning in the Mountains, before 1610   *oil on panel   6¾ × 8⅜ in.*
Brunswick, Herzog Anton Ulrich-Museum

JOHANN LISS The Quack, about 1617 (after an engraving by LUCAS VAN LEYDEN, 1523)
oil on canvas   50¾ × 38¼ in.
Bremen, Kunsthalle

JOACHIM VON SANDRART Portrait of Johann Maximilian zum Jungen, 1636
oil on canvas 74⅜×53⅜ in.
Frankfurt-am-Main, Historisches Museum

PAUL TROGER The Assumption of St. John Nepomuk, 1750
oil on canvas 212½ × 137⅞ in.
Vienna, Österreichische Galerie, on loan from the Schottenstift

MATTHÄUS GÜNTHER   The Adoration of the Lamb (sketch for a ceiling painting) about 1750-60
oil on canvas   34¼ × 25 in.
Augsburg, Städtische Galerie

FRANZ ANTON MAULBERTSCH   The Victory of St. James over the Saracens (sketch for a ceiling painting) 1765
oil on cardboard   12½ × 18⅞ in.
Vienna, Österreichische Galerie

J. H. W. TISCHBEIN Portrait of Goethe in the Campagna, 1787 *oil on canvas* $64\frac{5}{8} \times 81\frac{1}{8}$ *in.*
Frankfurt-am-Main, Städelsches Kunstinstitut

CASPAR DAVID FRIEDRICH Polar Picture with W. E. Parry's "Griper", 1819 (generally known as The Wreck of the Hoffnung) 1824
oil on canvas 38⅝ × 50⅜ in.
Hamburg, Kunsthalle

PHILIPP OTTO RUNGE The Parents of the Artist, 1806 *oil on canvas* $76\frac{3}{8} \times 51\frac{1}{4}$ *in.*
Hamburg, Kunsthalle

JOSEPH ANTON KOCH The Schmadribach Fall, 1811 *oil on canvas* *48 × 36¾ in.*
Leipzig, Museum of Fine Arts

JULIUS SCHNORR VON CAROLSFELD The Visit of the Family of St. John to the Family of Christ, 1818
oil on canvas   48 × 40½ in.
Dresden, Gemäldegalerie

KARL BLECHEN The Ironworks at Eberswalde, about 1834   *oil on panel   9⅜ × 12¼ in.*
West Berlin, Staatliche Museen

ADOLF VON MENZEL The Room with the Balcony, 1845 *oil on cardboard* $22\frac{7}{8} \times 18\frac{1}{2}$ *in.*
West Berlin, Staatliche Museen

ANSELM FEUERBACH Iphigenia, 1871 *oil on canvas* $75\frac{5}{8} \times 49\frac{1}{4}$ *in.*
Stuttgart, Staatsgalerie

WILHELM LEIBL Three Women in Church, 1881 *oil on panel* $51\frac{3}{8} \times 30\frac{3}{8}$ *in.*
Hamburg, Kunsthalle

Drawings

BAVARIA St. Dorothy, about 1410-25 *woodcut* $10\frac{5}{8} \times 7\frac{1}{2}$ *in.*
Munich, Staatliche Graphische Sammlung

MASTER E. S.   The Virgin and Child of Einsiedeln, 1466   *engraving* $8\frac{3}{8} \times 5$ *in.*
Dresden, Kupferstichkabinett, et al.

MARTIN SCHONGAUER St. Anthony Tormented by Demons, about 1475 *engraving* $12\frac{3}{8} \times 9\frac{1}{8}$ *in.*
London, British Museum, et al.

ALBRECHT DÜRER View of Innsbruck, 1494 *watercolor* $5 \times 7\frac{3}{8}$ *in.*
Vienna, Albertina

ALBRECHT DÜRER   The Four Riders of the Apocalypse: from "The Apocalypse," 1498
woodcut   15½ × 11 in.
London, British Museum, et al.

ALBRECHT DÜRER Adam and Eve, 1504 *engraving* $10 \times 7\frac{5}{8}$ *in.*
London, British Museum, et al.

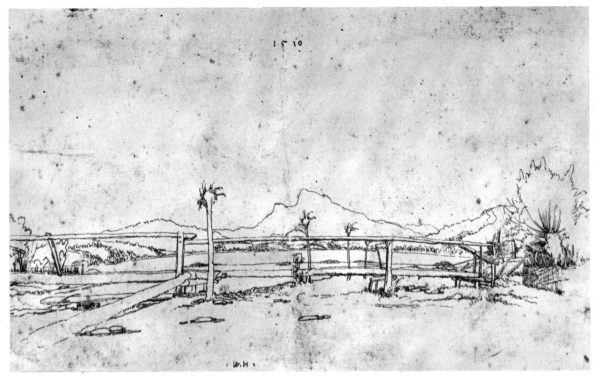

WOLF HUBER The Mondsee and Schafberg in Austria, 1510 *pen and ink 5 × 8¼ in.*
Nuremberg, Germanisches Nationalmuseum

HANS HOLBEIN the YOUNGER Lansquenets Fighting, 1530-32 *pen and wash 11¼ × 17⅜ in.*
Basel, Kunstmuseum

ALBRECHT DÜRER The Artist's Mother, 1514 *charcoal 16⅝ × 11⅞ in.*
West Berlin, Kupferstichkabinett

HANS HOLBEIN the YOUNGER Burgomaster Jakob Meyer, 1516
silverpoint and red chalk 10⅝ × 7½ in.
Basel, Kunstmuseum

HANS BURGKMAIR Emperor Maximilian Visiting the Artist's Studio: from "The Weisskunig," 1516 *woodcut* $8\frac{5}{8} \times 7\frac{5}{8}$ in.
West Berlin, Kupferstichkabinett

NIKLAS MANUEL (DEUTSCH) St. Christopher
pen and wash $7\frac{1}{4} \times 4\frac{5}{8}$ *in.*
Bern, Kunstmuseum

ADAM ELSHEIMER Landscape with a Caravan of Mules, about 1605 *pen and wash* $5\frac{3}{4} \times 6\frac{7}{8}$ *in.*
West Berlin, Kupferstichkabinett

EGID QUIRIN ASAM   Design for a Round Chapel, 1730
pen and watercolor with white highlights   19¾ × 14¾ in.
Munich, Staatliche Graphische Sammlung

ASMUS JAKOB CARSTENS Night with her Children, Sleep and Death, 1795 *black with white highlights* $29\frac{3}{8} \times 38\frac{3}{4}$ *in.*
Weimar, Schlossmuseum

ALFRED RETHEL Death the Rider: from
"Another Dance of Death," 1849 *woodcut* $8\frac{5}{8} \times 12\frac{5}{8}$ *in.*
Aachen, Suermondt Museum, et al.

ADOLF VON MENZEL Evening Meal at
Sanssouci: from Franz Kugler's
"The Life of Frederick the Great," 1840
wood engraving $5\frac{1}{2} \times 4$ *in.*
West Berlin, Kupferstichkabinett, et al.

LUDWIG ADRIAN RICHTER
Glory to God in the Highest: from "Picturesque and
Romantic Germany," 1855
woodcut $12\frac{7}{8} \times 10\frac{3}{4}$ *in.*
Dresden, Kupferstichkabinett, et al.

ADOLF VON MENZEL   Studies of Suits of Armor, 1866   *gouache* $17\frac{3}{8} \times 22\frac{5}{8}$ *in.*
Hamburg, Kunsthalle

Sculpture

RHINELAND   The Gero Cross, about 970
polychromed wood   height 73⅝ in.
Cologne, Cathedral

COLOGNE   The Madonna and Child, 973-982   *gold on wood   height 29¼ in.*
Essen, Cathedral

LOWER SAXONY Doors: Scenes from the Old and New
Testaments, 1008-15
bronze relief   height 185⅞ in.
Hildesheim, Cathedral

FRANCONIA   Jonas and Hosea, about 1235   *stone   under life size*
Bamberg, Cathedral

THURINGIA Eckehart and Uta, about 1250-60 *stone   over life size*
Naumburg, Cathedral

BOHEMIA? The Madonna and Child from Krumau, about 1400
polychromed stone height 44⅛ in.
Vienna, Kunsthistorisches Museum

HANS MULTSCHER   The Man of Sorrows and the
Virgin, 1429   *stone   height 67⅜ in.*
Ulm, Parish Church

TILMAN RIEMENSCHNEIDER   The Last Supper: from The Altar of the Holy Blood, 1504
wood   height 96⅛ in.
Rothenburg, St. Jakob

GREGOR ERHART   The Madonna of Mercy, about 1515
polychromed and gilded wood   height 72⅞ in.
Frauenstein, Austria, Parish Church

VEIT STOSS   The Annunciation, 1518   *polychromed wood   height about 156 in.*
Nuremberg, St. Lorenz

HANS LEINBERGER Count Albrecht of Hapsburg, 1518:
from The Tomb of Emperor Maximilian I *bronze over life size*
Innsbruck, Hofkirche

PETER VISCHER King Arthur, 1513:
from The Tomb of Emperor Maximilian I *bronze over life size*
Innsbruck, Hofkirche

HANS REICHLE St. Michael and Lucifer, 1606 *bronze* *height about 180 in.*
Augsburg, Armory

ANDREAS SCHLÜTER   Monument to the Elector of Brandenburg, 1696-1709   *bronze   over life size*
West Berlin, Charlottenburg Palace

EGID QUIRIN ASAM   The Assumption of the Virgin: from the High Altar, 1722   *plaster   over life size*
Rohr, Bavaria, Monastery Church

GEORG RAPHAEL DONNER The Judgment of Paris, about 1730 *bronze relief* $23\frac{5}{8} \times 38\frac{1}{4}$ *in.*
Vienna, Österreichische Galerie

JOHANN GOTTFRIED SCHADOW
Princesses Luise and Friederike of Prussia, 1795   *marble   height 67¾ in.*
East Berlin, Staatliche Museen

Influences and Developments

a

Early German Art

The finest surviving examples of early German art are small pieces—jewelry, crowns, crosses (a), book covers (b), shrines (c)—in gold and silver, ivory, enamels, and precious stones. These treasures were too expensive for any patrons but sovereigns and the greater churches. The meticulous figures on the shrines of the Romanesque goldsmiths had as impressive a monumentality as the stone sculpture of the time.

b

a Cologne
The Lothar Cross, about 1000
gold and silver-gilt, precious stones, and enamel on wood 19⅝ × 15¼ *in.*
Aachen, Cathedral

b Essen?
Cover of the Gospels of Abbess Theophanu, about 1039-1056
gold relief, ivory, and precious stones 14 × 10¼ *in.*
Essen, Cathedral

c Nicholas of Verdun and his Cologne Workshop
Shrine of the Three Kings, about 1181-1230
gold and silver-gilt relief, enamel, and precious stones on wood 70⅞ × 43¼ × 66⅞ *in.*
Cologne, Cathedral

c

Free-standing Sculpture

The earliest free-standing sculptures of medieval Europe are found in Germany. The symbolic bronze *Lion* at Brunswick (a) commemorated temporal power and privilege. Later monuments were of men, but these sculptures were still forceful symbols of independence (c), or of the knightly ideal (b), rather than memorial likenesses of individuals. The 14th-century images carved as aids to devotion in this age of mysticism and new awareness of Christ's sufferings (d, e) were both spiritual and poignant.

a

b

c

d

e

a Brunswick?
The Brunswick Lion, 1166
bronze, originally gilded life size
Brunswick, Castle Square

b Franconia
The Bamberg Rider, about 1237
stone
Bamberg, Cathedral

c Thuringia
The Magdeburg Rider, Monument to Emperor Otto II, about 1250
stone life size
Magdeburg, Old Market
(now in the Cathedral)

d Swabia
Christ and St. John, about 1320
polychromed and gilded wood
$35 \times 17\frac{3}{4}$ *in.*
West Berlin, Staatliche Museen

e Central Germany
Pietà, about 1340
wood $66\frac{7}{8} \times 41\frac{3}{4} \times 22\frac{1}{2}$ in.
Erfurt, Ursuline Convent

146

The Rise of the Graphic Arts

In 15th-century Germany the print became popular as a quick and cheap means of expounding religion and morality. Woodcuts were manufactured both as single sheets and as book illustrations (a), anonymously and in bulk. The popular woodcut illustrations of the 16th century (b, c, d) were inexhaustibly inventive. It was not long before copper engravings became equally popular. Among the earliest of them are 47 playing-cards in suits of birds (e), flowers, animals, and savages.

c

a

b

d

e

a Bamberg
The Widower before Death: from
"The Farmer from Bohemia"
woodcut $8\frac{1}{4} \times 5\frac{1}{4}$ *in.*
Wolfenbüttel, Herzog-August Bibliothek

b Hans Holbein the Younger
Death and the Astronomer, from
"The Dance of Death," 1523-24
woodcut $2\frac{1}{4} \times 2$ *in.*
Basel, Kunstmuseum, et al.

c Jost Amman
The Sculptor: from
"The True Description of All
Estates," 1568
woodcut $3\frac{1}{8} \times 2\frac{3}{8}$ *in.*
London, British Museum, et al.

d Tobias Stimmer
The Brazen Serpent: from
"New Illustrations of Bible
Stories," 1576
woodcut $6\frac{1}{4} \times 5\frac{1}{4}$ *in.*
London, British Museum, et al.

e Master of the Playing Cards
Five of Birds: playing card,
about 1440
engraving $5\frac{3}{8} \times 3\frac{7}{8}$ *in.*
*Munich, Staatliche Graphische
Sammlung, et al.*

Grünewald and Niclas Hagnower
The Isenheim Altarpiece
about 1505-1515
oil on wood and polychromed wood
132¼ × 231⅞ in.
Colmar, France, Unterlinden Museum

a with wings closed:
St. Anthony;
The Crucifixion;
St. Sebastian;
The Deposition (predella panel)

b with the first pair of wings opened:
The Annunciation;
The "Christmas Picture";
The Resurrection

c with second pair of wings opened:
St. Anthony's Visit to St. Paul;
St. Anthony, St. Augustine,
St. Jerome;
The Temptation of St. Anthony;
Christ and the Twelve Disciples
(predella panels)

The Altarpiece: the Focus of German Art

When a patron had decided on the subject, painters, carvers, joiners, and other craftsmen combined to create elaborate winged altarpieces like the one that Grünewald and the sculptor Niclas Hagnower made for the wealthy Isenheim Monastery in Alsace. As the huge wings unfold (a, b,c) the stories unfold too, like scenes in a sacred play. St. Anthony dominates the painting and sculpture of the altarpiece just as he presided over the monastery and its hospital. His lament—"Where were you, good Jesus?"—is on the horrifying *Temptation* panel (c). Carved, "architectural" altarpieces were another German specialty. The early Baroque altar (d) has the same format and slender monstrance-like shape as the Gothic design of a century earlier (e).

d Jörg Zürn
High Altar, 1616
wood with some gilding
Überlingen, St. Nikolaus

e Swabia
Design for an altarpiece, about 1500
pen on paper 27¼ × 11 in.
Ulm, Stadtbibliothek

d

e

New Patrons

Simple, silver objects for use in private houses began to find a wide market in the 13th century, but two centuries elapsed before the middle classes grew rich or leisured enough to compete with palaces and church treasuries in the luxury of gold and jewelry. Merchants in the late Gothic period commissioned goblets, rings, chains, and even bridal crowns, for their families, and cups or beakers for the better enjoyment of their guild sessions. Side by side with these innovations on the goldsmiths' workbenches, exquisite church furnishings (a) continued to be made as before, until the Reformation reduced the demand for liturgical ornament. Goldsmiths then worked almost solely for the wealthy connoisseur and indulged the Renaissance taste for motifs from nature. Goblet stems were twisted into the form of naturalistic tree trunks (c); the bowl and base might be ornamented with flowers, fruit, or animals. The sensuous alabaster *Judith* by Conrad Meyt (b) is one of the finest small sculptures of the northern Renaissance.

a

b

c

A New Subject: the Individual

The Romanesque artist was himself a humble member of a monastery, cathedral workshop, or stoneyard, and little interested in the individual as a subject of his art. It is no accident that the earliest realistic self-portrait in medieval Europe (a) was by Peter Parler, one of the first architect-sculptors to emerge as a distinct artistic personality. His bust is one of a lifelike series in Prague Cathedral, where Emperor Charles IV, for whom the cathedral was built, and the builders themselves are also represented. Gothic patrons began to demand a place in the sacred works they commissioned; hence the practice of incorporating the figure of the donor in adoration before the main subject of an altarpiece. It was thus that the full-length portrait evolved as an art form. An early pair (b), once wings of an altarpiece of the Crucifixion, call to mind Dürer's definition: "The art of painting is performed in the service of the Church. It demonstrates the sufferings of Our Lord, and preserves the image of man beyond death."

During the northern Renaissance, men of influence who wished their portraits to be widely known ordered bronze medals (c), like those already fashionable in Italy, and distributed them in quantity. Luther's partisan, Lucas Cranach the Elder, exploited the print, the other great medium of mass production, in portrait engravings (d) and woodcuts of the reformer.

a

b

c

d

a Peter Parler
Self-portrait, about 1380
stone   under life size
Prague, Cathedral

b Jerg Ratgeb
Claus Stalburg and his Wife:
from an altarpiece, 1504
oil on wood   74⅜ × 22 in. each
Frankfurt-am-Main, Städelsches
Kunstinstitut

c Hans Schwarz
Count Palatine Georg, Bishop of
Speyer, 1520
bronze 2⅝ in. diameter
Munich, Staatliche Münzsammlung, et al.

d Lucas Cranach the Elder
Martin Luther, 1521
engraving 8¼ × 5⅞ in.
London, British Museum, et al.

a

New Media

Mezzotint, porcelain, and lithography were three art forms developed in Germany and quickly carried throughout Europe in the 17th, 18th, and 19th centuries respectively.

Mezzotint engraving (a) was invented in 1642 by Ludwig von Siegen, a Hessian military officer, and taken to England by another amateur artist, Prince Rupert of the Rhine. English engravers became particularly skilled in their use of this medium, which enabled them to achieve a close approximation to the textures of painting. Mezzotinters needed patience and experience with their fragile plates. Lithography (b), a printing method based on the water-repellent property of grease, is rapid, simple, and cheap. Invented in 1798 by an unsuccessful German dramatist, Aloys Senefelder, it was developed and patented by him and excelled in by the French, especially by Daumier and Toulouse-Lautrec. However, in the art of the porcelain figure (c), Germany's brilliant court factories, like that established in 1710 at Meissen, have always retained their supremacy.

b

a Ludwig von Siegen
   Amelia Elisabeth of Hesse, 1643
   mezzotint 14¼ × 12⅜ in.
   London, British Museum, et al.

b Wilhelm Reuter
   Head of a Girl, about 1810
   lithograph 8¼ × 7¼ in.
   Mannheim, Kunsthalle, et al.

c Johann Joachim Kändler
   Harlequin and Columbine, 1740
   porcelain (Meissen) height 7¼ in.
   Dresden, Porzellansammlung

c

SPANISH ART
TO 1900

Edited, with an Introduction, by

Dr. Xavier de Salas

Deputy Director, Museo del Prado, Madrid

Introduction

Spanish Art to 1900

After the collapse of the Roman Empire in the 5th century A. D., the Visigoths crossed into the Iberian peninsula and founded a kingdom that lasted for more than 200 years. For most of this time they pursued a policy of assimilation with the Roman citizens who already inhabited what is now Spain and Portugal. When the Visigoths first arrived, their kings, though Christian, were Arian heretics, but they returned to orthodoxy in 587 and the integration of the invaders and the native peoples proceeded rapidly. In 711, however, the Moors from North Africa invaded Spain and, within four years, had reached the Pyrenees. They were decisively defeated in an attempt to invade France, but more than 700 years were to pass before the Christian people of Spain drove out the last of the Moorish invaders.

The whole of the Middle Ages in Spain, therefore, was taken up with the gradual reconquest of the Christian kingdoms which, by the beginning of the 15th century, consisted of Portugal, Castile, Aragón, and Navarre. The last Moslem kingdom, that of Granada, finally fell in 1492. By this time the two most powerful kingdoms, Aragón and Castile, had been united by the marriage of the Catholic monarchs Ferdinand and Isabella, so that by the beginning of the 16th century most of Spain was unified. The political and economic power conferred by the union of Aragón and Castile and the subsequent annexation of Navarre was further increased by the discovery of the Americas by Christopher Columbus in 1492. After the deaths of Isabella in 1504, and Ferdinand in 1516, their grandson Charles inherited enormous territories in northern Europe through his other grandfather, Emperor Maximilian of Austria. The new king of Spain was also Charles V, the nominal ruler of the Holy Roman Empire. His son, Philip II of Spain, thus boasted that the sun never set on his empire.

Moslem influences on Spanish art

Little remains of the early medieval painting that flourished in the north of Spain as in other parts of Europe, but there are many paintings of high quality in the Gothic style dating from late medieval times. The characteristics of Spanish painting will be discussed further on, but it must be pointed out that the Moslem conquerors inevitably left a deep impression on Spanish civilization, and the art of Spain has thus differed profoundly from that of any other European country. This is particularly evident in Spanish architecture, which cannot be understood without considering the centuries-long existence of Moslem art in the Iberian peninsula. Some of its most characteristic decorative forms persisted throughout successive Christian styles. It is equally true of the applied arts; even in the 18th century pottery was still being made in Valencia and elsewhere showing Moslem decorative forms when outstanding examples of Rococo porcelain were being produced at the Buen Retiro Palace in Madrid.

French influences were supreme at the Spanish court, and the newly founded Real Academia de San Fernando in Madrid, opened in 1752, advocated a style based both on French Rococo and on Italian-inspired Neoclassicism.

Spanish painting falls into a different category, for its forms are exclusively European. This is probably explained by the Moslem prohibition on the representation of the human figure, which meant that almost all Moslem artistic activity was confined to architecture and the arts of decoration. Much the same is true of sculpture, at least as far as free-standing figures are concerned. The relief carvings of the Moslem craftsmen were used almost entirely for decorative purposes, and their influence affected architecture but not representational sculpture.

Spanish painting

The development of painting in Europe was closely paralleled in Spain; such phenomena as the naturalistic movement in Italy at the beginning of the 17th century were adopted so rapidly and so extensively in Spain that they must have corresponded very closely to deeprooted Spanish artistic instincts; to a lesser extent this is also true of the Baroque style. The architecture of the buildings which housed these paintings, however, was more markedly influenced by an Eastern spirit altogether alien to the art of Italy or France, and most Spanish cathedrals can offer examples of these stylistic incongruities.

Early in the 14th century some Italian or Italian-trained painters introduced the new Tuscan style into Spain, first of all into Catalonia and Majorca, and then later into Castile. Both Castile and Aragón were influenced by the International Gothic style of the late 14th and early 15th centuries, since this style resulted from a conjunction of ideas and masters in Avignon at the time when the popes were resident there.

The extremely naturalistic art that developed in Flanders from the 1420's was in its turn adapted by Spanish painters, beginning in Castile. The greatest of the early Flemish masters, Jan van Eyck, who actually visited Portugal, exerted a strong influence, particularly on the work of Luis Dalmáu, for example *The Madonna of the Councilors* (p. 219). But by the beginning of the 16th century Italy rather than Flanders had become the model for Spanish painters.

The classical Renaissance style often filtered into Spain by way of Flanders, however, bringing with it much of the exaggeration and detail that characterizes northern Mannerism. The Flemish interest in popular genre subjects also formed a current in the Spanish tradition, and Spanish still-life painters seem to owe much to the example of Flemish or Dutch contemporaries. In the 16th century Italian Mannerism was enthusiastically adopted, and at least one Spanish sculptor, Alonso Berruguete, whose works include *Eve* and *Abraham and Isaac* (p. 277), was in Florence at the critical moment and was influenced by Michelangelo, like his Italian Mannerist contemporaries Rosso and Pontormo.

Italy continued to influence Spanish painters until the 18th century. The arrival of El Greco in Spain from Italy about 1577 was, however, an event of the greatest importance, for he became the most profound interpreter of the culture of his adopted country, in a language which was fundamentally that of Italian Mannerism, seen in *The Holy Trinity* (p. 229), *The Martyrdom of St. Maurice and the Theban Legion* (p. 230), *Cardinal Don Fernando Niño de Guevara* (p. 232), and *Laocöon* (p. 233).

The political domination of the Italian peninsula by the Spanish monarch began in the Middle Ages and was long continued, especially in the south, where the kingdom of Naples remained closely linked with Spain during the centuries. Therefore it is difficult to decide whether José de Ribera, who painted *The Martyrdom of St. Bartholomew* (p. 234) and *The Holy Trinity* (p. 235), should be regarded as a Spaniard working in Italy or a Spanish-born Italian painter whose works are almost indistinguishable from those of his Spanish contemporaries.

The Golden Age of painting

The 17th century was the age of three of the most outstanding personalities in Spanish painting, Velázquez, Zurbarán, and Murillo, who, by any standards, were three of the greatest artists of the century. All three owe something to Italy, but their own influences extended ultimately throughout Europe. Murillo's somewhat sentimental art, exemplified in *A Girl and her Duenna* (p. 246), was greatly admired in the 18th century. On the other hand, although Velázquez was admired in Rome during his brief visits from 1629 to 1631, and from 1648 to 1651, his serene and realistic art did not really become known and appreciated until the 19th century, when, following the Napoleonic wars, many of his works reached Paris and London. The same is true of Zurbarán, whose work became known in Europe at large as a result of the Napoleonic wars, and above all through the sale, in 1853, of the great collection of his works formed by King Louis Philippe of France, including *The Annunciation* (p. 244) and *The Immaculate Conception* (p. 243).

The 18th century

During the 18th century the Hapsburg dynasty was supplanted by the Bourbons and, as a result, several

French and Italian artists came to Spain and exerted great influence on the court. Some of the best European painters of the century worked in Madrid, including men as far apart stylistically as Anton Raphael Mengs and Giovanni Battista Tiepolo.

The Bourbon kings, like their predecessors, were great collectors and bought many works of art, especially in Italy. Unfortunately, the fire of 1734 at the Alcázar in Madrid destroyed many pictures, but enough survived in the royal collections to form one of the greatest assemblages of masterpieces in the world. The time was therefore ripe for the appearance of a great artist; there was a court with a taste for painting and the knowledge necessary for good patronage, and there were masterpieces available for study in the royal collection, as well as in the works of Mengs, Tiepolo, and other living artists.

Goya was this new genius. More than any other artist of the period it was he who started a new phase in European painting, so much so that he has been called, not without justification, the first modern painter. He himself said that his masters had been Velázquez, Rembrandt, and nature, but in fact Goya's art is a synthesis of many other styles. The Italian Late Baroque painters working in Madrid—Luca Giordano, Corrado Giaquinto, and above all, the greatest fresco painter of the century, Tiepolo—made a deep impression on Goya, while his portrait style reflected contemporary French and even English practice, as in *The Countess del Carpio* (p. 252), *The Family of Charles IV* (p. 253), and *Don Juan Bautista de Muquiro* (p. 255). He worked for years for the royal tapestry factory—*The Parasol* (p. 251) was one of his designs—where Mengs was the artistic director. Of even greater importance was Goya's study of Velázquez and the great Renaissance painters in the royal collection.

From all this, Goya's highly personal style anticipated most of the basic elements of both Impressionism and Expressionism. He disdained the conventional formulas of his day and forged for himself a style of a previously unknown intensity and imaginative quality.

The Royal Collections

The rulers of Spain had assembled one of the greatest collections of paintings that has ever existed and housed it in Madrid and the royal palaces near the capital.

Naturally, the Madrid School was most directly influenced by the examples provided by this collection, although they exerted a powerful and permanent influence over the whole country. It was after his study of Titian that Velázquez changed his palette and radically altered his whole style, even before he went to Italy, as *The Toilet of Venus* (p. 241) shows. Murillo also changed his style after seeing pictures by Barocci in the royal collection in Madrid; *The Dream of the Patrician* (p. 247) demonstrates this. Goya himself transformed his whole conception of painting after he began to work for the royal household and had access to the collections. Spanish painters were also profoundly influenced by engravings imported on a large scale from France, Flanders, and Italy. Many Spanish artists also visited Italy or France as part of their studies.

The Spanish colonies

The growth of a Spanish school so closely tied to those of Europe was made possible because of Spain's position as a great power. From about 1490 until the 18th century she was one of the dominant nations in Europe, reaching her apogee in the late 16th and early 17th centuries. During the reign of Philip II and his immediate successors the territories of the Spanish monarchy included large areas of Italy and the Low Countries, and even parts of France. She was enriched by supplies of silver from the American colonies which, until the end of the 18th century, extended from Texas and Florida southward to the Andes, except for Brazil, which was a Portuguese possession. Cuba, Puerto Rico, and the West Indies were also Spanish, as were the Philippines and other possessions in Africa and the Pacific.

Spain was the first European power to arrive on the American continent. The original Spanish colonies in North and South America were so immense that an understanding of Spanish art must also take into account the work of Spaniards in the American territories (Creoles), and especially of the *mestizos* (Spanish Indians).

From the 16th to the 19th centuries an enormous amount of building took place, each of the viceroys and captain-generals dotting his territory with cathedrals, churches, palaces, convents, and houses, as well as works of civil engineering such as fortifications and bridges. Not surprisingly, the rulers preferred architects who worked in the Spanish style and many of them commiss-ioned designs to be sent out from Spain. These designs were, however, usually adapted to suit local conditions. Sometimes they were freely interpreted by the colonial stonemasons and sculptors who had a strong local tra-dition of their own; sometimes the employment of different materials meant that the original design, though still basically Spanish, had a distinctively Ame-rican flavor. In so short a summary as this it is impossible to discuss this Hispano-American art and architecture in any detail, but it can be said that much of it stands in something of the same relationship to Spanish art as did the Roman provinces to the imperial capital. Roman art, though it rarely attained to the perfection and beauty of Greek art, had admirable qualities of strength, proportion, and splendor that were transmitted, albeit in simpler forms, to the provinces. Similarly, many of these Hispanic works were an interpretation of Euro-pean art; though less sophisticated, they occasionally reached a perfection of their own.

Some characteristics of Spanish art

From the Middle Ages to the time of Goya religious art was of primary importance. The ardor of the Spanish religious temperament is one of the mainsprings of all art in Spain, and is the key to the understanding of many of its characteristics. It is true that practically every painter of every European school in the Middle Ages was occupied almost exclusively with religious subjects. Beginning with the Renaissance in the 15th and 16th centuries, however, there was a general widening of sub-ject matter. The cult of antiquity and a new interest in classical mythology provided artists with many themes parallel to the older Christian subjects. Scenes from ordinary life became more important and, from being merely background subjects, often became the principal subjects of pictures.

In Spain, on the other hand, religious subjects con-tinued to the exclusion of almost everything else, except a few scenes of everyday life, military scenes, such as Velázquez's *Surrender of Breda* (p. 238), still-lifes, and, of course, portraits. Subjects from classical mytho-logy and paintings of the nude are rare in Spanish art. This was only partly on account of religious objections; more important was the fact that there was no prospe-rous middle class to buy such pictures, unlike the mer-chant families who had risen to power almost every-where else in Europe. Thus, the Spanish artist still relied on the church or the court. The aristocrats who made up the court tended to commission portraits and a few decorative subjects for their palaces, but it was the churches and convents that remained the greatest source of patronage.

Portrait painting and still-life

As elsewhere, portraits were extremely popular, but there was a certain characteristic Spanishness about them that arose from the passionate concern for indi-vidual characteristics rather than the ideal beauty that concerned Italian and other artists.

This profound interest in the individual led Spanish painters from the very early 17th century onward to the representation of things in everyday life, and special categories of still-life painting arose, so that *florero* is a recognized art term to describe flower paintings, and *bodegóne* is used for kitchen subjects depicting food, as in Meléndez's *Still-life* (p. 250), cooking utensils, or such typical genre scenes as Velázquez's *Old Woman Frying Eggs* (p. 237). These subjects are treated with a solemnity and intensity of observation which make Spanish still-life and genre paintings totally different from pictures of the same kind painted in northern Europe. They reveal a depth of perception toward mundane objects that arouses an emotional response in the spectator, since he is made to contemplate them as symbols of a deeper meaning.

Landscape painting

Rather surprisingly, this passionate concern for everyday surroundings was not extended to landscape. Landscape painting as such hardly existed in Spain. Spanish paint-ers generally relied on accepted formulas for decorative landscapes and produced imaginary and idealized sce-nery in the Italian or Flemish manner, or, in the 18th century, imitations of sophisticated French pastoral landscapes. This indifference to nature is simply a reflection of the general lack of interest in the natural sciences, which at this time were generally neglected in Spain, although cultivated in the rest of Europe.

In the depiction of outdoors scenes few Spanish painters bothered much over detail or accuracy. The great masters tended to express themselves with speed and fluency in a kind of shorthand which, because they were great masters, had an immediacy and vividness that more than compensated for lack of detail. In the hands of lesser men this lack of interest made for carelessness.

The cultivation of an intellectual ideal of beauty or proportion, as understood by the Italians and the French, was alien to most Spanish artists, who concentrated their efforts on intensity of expression, sacrificing everything else to this end. This obsessive quality resulted in hauntingly powerful works when it was successful, but the products of minor painters were often merely rhetorical.

Spanish naturalism

Except when depicting landscape, Spanish painters thus tended to express themselves in a highly naturalistic style. The detailed intensity with which they depicted the visible world gave an equally tangible reality to their representation of the supernatural world. From this arose the paradox of a deeply spiritual approach to religious painting expressed in terms of an intense, literal naturalism.

The Spaniard tends to assert his personality in some form of violence. In art this sometimes results in a monumental conception of figures in relation to their setting. The figures burst out of a dark background with a melodramatic spotlight effect, enthusiastically adopted from Caravaggio and his followers. Examples are Zurbarán's *Death of S. Bonaventura* (p. 242), and Ribera's *St. Agnes in Prison* (p. 236). Because of this intensity of light and shadow, color tended to be less important. Throughout the 16th and 17th centuries most Spanish artists used a very somber palette consisting of the earth colors, dull yellow, browns, olive greens, and brownish reds, as well as black. These dark tones were set off by the gold of the decorative frames surrounding most of the works.

The fashion for dressing in black, which was characteristic of Spain in the 16th and 17th centuries, had its own effect on portraiture, seen in El Greco's *Burial of Count Orgaz* (p. 231). Sobriety of color remained the rule until the triumph of the Rococo style in the 18th century; until then a gravity of pose and a dark, austere color scheme gave an air of family resemblance to all portraits, as in Goya's *Countess del Carpio, Marchioness of Solana* (p. 252).

Many of these characteristics lasted unchanged for centuries. When changes did come the rhythm tended to be very slow. Thus, the Gothic style persisted for centuries in Spanish cathedrals, some of which, such as those of Segovia and Salamanca, were completed only during the Renaissance. These are extreme cases, but the persistence of a medieval spirit can be found in many examples in all the arts.

On the other hand, one or two of the greatest masters actually anticipated stylistic changes in the rest of Europe. Velázquez represented space in terms of tone, as in *The Maids of Honor* (p. 239) and *View of Granada* (p. 261), and this exact perspective of tones throughout the picture provided a solution to problems which had concerned his predecessors and his contemporaries—a solution not fully understood or appreciated until centuries after his death. In his mature works, such as *The Second of May*, Goya created a style that was close to the intentions of many of the greatest European artists of the 19th century.

Biographies

SOME BOOKS FOR FURTHER READING

W. Stirling-Maxwell, *Annals of the Artists of Spain*, 5 vols.,
    London, 1891.
C. R. Post, *A History of Spanish Painting*, 12 vols., Cam-
    bridge, Mass., 1930-58.
B. Bevan, *History of Spanish Architecture*, London, 1938.
M. Gómez-Moreno, *Brief History of Spanish Sculpture*,
    Madrid, 1957.
G. Kubler and M. Soria, *Art and Architecture in Spain and
    Portugal and their American Dominions, 1500-1800*,
    (Pelican History of Art) London, 1959.

SEE ALSO UNDER THE INDIVIDUAL BIOGRAPHIES

FERRER BASSA   about 1285-1348

The Giotto of Spanish painting

Three kings of Aragón in turn employed Ferrer Bassa, who was from Sasgaioles
near Barcelona. He was already valued as a painter at the court when in 1320 he
was pardoned by King James II for a serious, but unspecified, crime. Soon afterwards he was busy painting in various castles and convents in Catalonia, Aragón,
and Valencia. In 1333 he began for Alfonso IV the illumination of a manuscript
book called "The Usages of Barcelona and the Customs of Catalonia." This took
more than a year to finish, and was accomplished enough for the next king,
Pedro IV, to write to his queen in 1342 requesting a book of hours illuminated by Ferrer Bassa. Pedro IV made Bassa his court painter, and also employed
him on diplomatic missions. At some time during his reign, which began in 1336,
Bassa seems to have made a journey to the papal court at Avignon. There he met
the Sienese painter Simone Martini and saw the work that he was doing from
about 1335.

In 1345, Bassa signed a contract with the abbess to paint murals in the convent
at Pedralbes in the suburbs of Barcelona. These murals are his only remaining
work, and almost the last he executed. They were finished by November, 1346. At
the end of 1348, while working in the Franciscan Monastery at Valencia, Bassa
died. He left a son, Arnaldo, also a painter, and a daughter, who married a well-
known sculptor, Jaime Castayls.

The nuns at Pedralbes eventually built tall, wooden linen cupboards on the
walls of the little chapel that Bassa had decorated from ceiling to floor. At the
beginning of the 20th century the cupboards were taken down and the murals were
found in an excellent state of preservation. Simone Martini and the artistic atmosphere at Avignon made a deep impression on Bassa as did the work of other
contemporary Italian painters, Giotto in Florence, Duccio in Siena, and the half
Sienese, half Florentine Lorenzetti brothers. Books illuminated with miniatures by
Italian painters were circulating in Spain, and Bassa was aware of contemporary
developments in Italy. In his work there are compositions taken straight from the
Sienese, like the formal rows of angels in *The Madonna Enthroned,* and an over-all
directness of design derived from Giotto. The oval-faced people that gaze mysti-
cally from Bassa's work through their strange narrow, slanting eyes are typical of
the contemporary Sienese style.

A feeling for the observable and natural in an attitude, an expression, or the
hang of a garment, which was to persist through all Spanish painting, enabled
Bassa to attain a simplification completely unlike the meticulous, detailed graceful-
ness of the contemporary Sienese style. Simplification of surfaces gave solidity to
his forms, and movement to his attitudes. It lent an emotion to facial expressions
that is most remarkable in the brutal scenes of *The Passion* in the Pedralbes
murals.

C. Zervos Catalan Art London, 1937
E. Harris Spanish Painting London, 1938

S. Marcisius, about 1346
*Pedralbes, Convent of the Nuns of
the Order of St. Clare, St. Michael's Chapel*

HIS WORKS INCLUDE

Cycle of Murals, 1345-46
*Pedralbes, Convent of the Nuns of
the Order of St. Clare, St. Michael's Chapel*
The Nativity, about 1346
*Pedralbes, Convent of the Nuns of
the Order of St. Clare, St. Michael's Chapel*

See also page 217

The Three Marys at the Tomb,
about 1346
*Pedralbes, Convent of the Nuns of
the Order of St. Clare, St. Michael's Chapel*

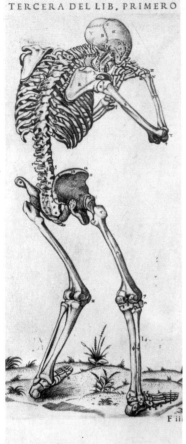

Skeleton, about 1555
Madrid, Bibl. Nac.

GASPAR BECERRA 1520-1570

An artist more interesting for his varied enthusiasms than for the beauty of his work

Gaspar Becerra was born in Baéza, Jaén province, in 1520, son of the mediocre painter Antonio Becerra and Leonor Padilla. It was natural that he should try to better his father's achievements, and so he left for Italy about 1540. In 1545, he worked as assistant to Vasari on paintings for the Chancellery in Rome, and from 1550 to 1555 he collaborated with Daniele da Volterra on frescoes in the Church of S. Trinità dei Monti. At that time he also produced illustrations for "The Anatomy" by Doctor John of Valverde, published in Rome in 1556. These illustrations demonstrate his knowledge of the human body and his zeal in investigation.

Becerra returned to Spain and married Paula Velázquez on July 15, 1556. He began a period of intense work in the manner of the typical Renaissance artist, as an architect, painter, and sculptor, executing commissions with varying degrees of success. In Madrid his activities centered around works for royalty, and in the Alcázar he painted frescoes in company with Juan Bautista Castello and Romulo Cincinato. This building is now destroyed, and his important remaining frescoes, 1562-63, relating the story of Danaë and Perseus, are in the Palace of El Pardo. These pictures are reminiscent of the Italianate style of Francesco Parmigianino, but are more notable for historical interest than for their intrinsic beauty.

In 1563 Becerra was appointed court painter. However, he is better known for his drawings. *The Polyphemus* and his copy of Michelangelo's *Last Judgment* testify to his constant and lively interest in classical literature and Italian art, of which he himself was a belated offshoot. Nevertheless, his best drawing is of the great altarpiece in the Monastery of Descalzas Reales in Madrid. Becerra died in Madrid in 1570.

M. Gómez-Moreno   Renaissance Sculpture in Spain   Paris, 1931

HIS WORKS INCLUDE

The High Altar, 1558-60
Astorga, Cath.

The High Altar, 1563
Madrid, Monastery of Descalzas Reales

Jesus Descending from the Cross, 1563
Madrid, Boix Coll.

See also page 259

St. Mary Magdalen
Madrid, Prado

ALONSO BERRUGUETE   about 1489-1561

The most individual and talented sculptor of the Spanish Renaissance

Alonso Berruguete was born in Paredes de Nava in Castile. His father was the great painter Pedro Berruguete and his mother was Doña Elvira González. The exact date of his birth is unknown, but in 1504 he went to Italy, as his father had done. He stayed in Florence, and also in Rome, where he was outshone by the dazzling genius of Michelangelo, who took him under his wing.

In 1518 he returned to Spain and one of his first commissions was the tomb of Chancellor Selvagio, for the Church of S. Engracia in Saragossa. Failing to gain favor with Emperor Charles V, Berruguete settled down in Valladolid, where he was soon acclaimed as a sculptor, rather than as a painter as he had hoped. He married Doña Juana de Pereda, and in 1525 he completed the altarpiece of the Church of La Mejorada in which he shows his expressive force, almost furious in its spontaneity. Another great work was the altarpiece of the Church of St. Benedict in Valladolid which he started in 1527 – an enormous series of reliefs and sculptures, among which are some of the most impressive figures of Spanish sculpture. In 1539 he was summoned to Toledo to help with the work on the high altar of the cathedral.

In his long Toledan period, Berruguete worked on the altarpiece of the Church of St. Ursula and on a final and most exclusive task, the tomb with the recumbent alabaster statue of Cardinal Don Juan de Tavera in the church of the Hospital of St. John the Baptist. It was a most daring work, for the ecclesiastic's face is shown, not as in life, but with the unmistakable gaping jaws of death, a forerunner of other macabre works in Spanish art. This tomb was his last work, and he died in Toledo at the end of September, 1561.

Berruguete, typical of the Renaissance artist in his twin roles of mediocre painter and brilliant sculptor, was an impressive character. Proud, highly sensitive, and a great friend of both bureaucrats and aristocrats, he still retained much of his youthful enthusiasm inspired by Michelangelo. This enthusiasm appeared frequently in his works, and sometimes gave a rough-shod appearance to his creation. As a sculptor in painted wood he created *St. Sebastian* and *Abraham and Isaac* for the altarpiece of St. Benedict, Valladolid. Another medium which Berruguete was fond of using was plain, uncolored wood, and some of his carvings in the choir at Toledo Cathedral, such as the graceful *Eve* and the thoughtful *St. John the Baptist*, figure among the most noble of his creations.

M. Gómez-Moreno   Renaissance Sculpture in Spain   Paris, 1931

The Transfiguration (detail)
about 1548
Toledo, Cath.

HIS WORKS INCLUDE

The Resurrection, about 1517
Valencia, Cath.

St. Sebastian, 1527-33
Valladolid, Mus.

Moses, choir stall, 1539-43
Toledo, Cath.

See also pages 258, 277

163

PEDRO BERRUGUETE

about 1450-1504

A Painter at the courts of Italy and Spain

Self-portrait (detail)
Madrid, Mus. Lázaro

Pedro Berruguete was born at Paredes de Nava in Castile, where his Basque grandfather had settled. Not far south in Palencia, Fernando Gallego was painting, and it is possible that Berruguete learned from him his expertise in the mixed Spanish-Flemish style which Gallego had made popular in Castile, and which other artists were establishing all over Spain. He learned to use oil as well as tempera, and to give a miniaturist's attention to the execution of every detail.

Berruguete's quick mastery of these techniques was noticed by the uncle after whom he was named, an influential Dominican monk. He arranged for him to go to Italy in the service of the pope. In Urbino about 1472 he received a commission from Duke Federico da Montefeltro to paint the duke's hand into a picture which Piero della Francesca had left unfinished when he began to write his theses on perspective and mathematics. After this, as "Pedro the Spaniard," Berruguete stayed on in Urbino Castle until his patron's death in 1482. He collaborated with Luca Signorelli and Melozzo da Forli, Francesca's successors as court painters. When the duke decided to employ the best living artists on a long series of oils of famous men, including prophets, philosophers, and the duke himself, he chose Berruguete and the Fleming, Joos van Ghent.

In 1483 Berruguete was back in Spain. His style had acquired a sophisticated Italian overlay. In his new relaxed confidence, faces assumed character, male figures vitality, and female ones grace. Over the next 16 years Berruguete painted frescoes in Toledo Cathedral, but only two are preserved. His first commission, in 1483 on his return to Spain, was murals for the sanctuary chapel. For some reason he left them half done, and in July, 1488, had to give a formal assurance that he would finish the task he had undertaken.

All this time Berruguete lived either in Paredes de Nava, where he also did some paintings, or in Toledo. Meanwhile, his uncle was in touch with the Inquisitor-General Tomás Torquemada, who was staying during the 1490's at the great Dominican Monastery of St. Thomas at Avilá and planning a scheme of decorations. The result was that in 1499 Berruguete went to Avilá, where he painted his masterpieces, the altarpieces of *St. Thomas, St. Dominic,* and *St. Peter Martyr.* The Spanish, Flemish, and Italian elements of his work fused with each other into a new, consistent art. The mastery of architectural perspective, which he had inherited from his Flemish-inspired training, and the differentiation of faces in crowds, which he had learned in Italy, gave meaning to his own Spanish realism, his love of extra, arbitrary, but natural, detail.

The *St. Thomas* altarpiece brought Berruguete's reputation to its height. In 1502, Philip the Fair, husband of the heiress to the throne, saw a small painting of *St. John the Evangelist on Patmos* done by Berruguete for his mother-in-law, Queen Isabella. He promptly made Berruguete his court painter, and raised him and his descendants to the nobility.

In the late 1480's, long enough after his return from Italy for him to have won considerable esteem in Spain, he married Elvira González, the daughter of a rich nobleman. They had six children of whom the eldest, called Alonso, was born about 1489 at Paredes de Nava. He became a pupil of his father and eventually the greatest and most vital sculptor of the Spanish Renaissance. Berruguete died on January 5, 1504, while still engaged on work for Avilá Cathedral.

C. R. Post A History of Spanish Painting, Vol. IX Cambridge, Mass., 1930-58
J. Lassaigne Spanish Painting, Vol. I Geneva, 1952

Panel of Salvator Mundi (detail) 1501
Guaza de Campos, Parish Church

St. Dominic and the Albigenses (detail)
Madrid, Prado

LUIS BORRASSÁ   about 1360 - after 1424

An original painter in a stagnating Catalan tradition

At the end of the 14th century there were several members of the Borrassá family painting in Catalonia. Luis was the teacher of some of them, and the best of all. He was born at Gerona about 1360, the year his father Guillermo began a lifetime of work at the cathedral there. 20 years later Luis himself was repairing its stained glass—a comparatively unskilled labor in contemporary eyes—while making a

St. Peter Walking on the Water, 1411
Tarrasa, S. María

small name as a painter. Within another eight years he was a popular painter in Barcelona with his own establishment.

With Pedro Serra in the Barcelona studio of the Serra brothers, Borrassá learned a great deal about new developments. He then developed Serra's style, following the international trends of the period. This resulted in a personal interpretation of the International Gothic style. From the Serras he learned to be delicate in the Italian manner, and to be clever with detail. He himself added what was eventually to be particularly characteristic of Spanish art—the power of close observation. Lighting, shading, and even foreshortening was more natural for Borrassá than for his contemporaries. Conventional compositions and expressions of figures and faces no longer seemed the only possibilities. He interspersed heavenly processions with human beings, and introduced everyday gestures and contemporary dress into religious subjects. He adopted for his soldiers and his executioners the fierce facial distortions which had invigorated Ferrer Bassa's work 50 years before. In Borrassá's last painting, *The St. Michael Altar*, there is, for the first time in his work and in Spanish painting, the suggestion of strong movement. Thus, his power of observation animated the substance of his work, while a brilliant range of color gave it surface vitality.

The king of Aragón, and churches and religious houses from all over Catalonia, showered Borrassá with contracts. He went to Saragossa to design some of the decorations for the coronation of Juan I. He sent out altar paintings to Guardiola, Tarrasa, Vich, Seva, and his home town of Gerona.

In 1413 there were disputes between the archdeacon of the Barcelona Church of S. María del Mar and his clergy. It is recorded that Borrassá, with other respected parishioners, was called on to witness the settlement. He died some time after 1424.

C. Zervos   Catalan Art   London, 1937

Altar of Guardiola, 1404
Barcelona, Mus. of Art

FRANCISCO CAMILO

about 1625-1673

An interesting painter and draftsman of Madrid

Francisco Camilo was born in Madrid about 1625, the son of Domenico Camilo of Florence and Doña Clara Pérez. After his father's death, his mother married Pedro de las Cuevas, a highly conscientious teacher of many famous painters of the Madrid School. He also taught Camilo, who had shown a precocious talent, and at 18 had completed a painting for the altarpiece of the Jesuit church in Madrid. It was a success, and caused other religious institutions to solicit his services. There was, however, a more important client, Philip IV, who commissioned him with a share of portraits of Spanish monarchs and a mural in the Buen Retiro, illustrating passages from Ovid's "Metamorphoses." He incurred some comments from the king, who was convinced that Camilo had depicted heroes of the myths with the same faces as his Christian figures. Although the major part of his work was stiff and formal, Camilo's undeniable gifts of good composition and warm colors were clearly visible.

It would not be possible to evaluate correctly the artistic worth of Camilo without referring to his sketches. Their precise drawing reveals his desire to succeed in the final paintings for which they were made. In the majority of cases, he did not sketch details, but the whole composition. Unfortunately, all that has survived of Camilo's work is of a religious nature. Thus, his classical and mythological subjects, so rare in the great paintings of the Madrid School of the 17th century, can only be imagined. Camilo died in Madrid in 1673.

A. de Beruete y Moret   The School of Madrid   London and New York, 1911

The Martyrdom of St. Bartholomew
Madrid, Prado

HIS WORKS INCLUDE

Christ and The Virgin Crowning St. Juan de Dios with Thorns, 1650
Barnard Castle, Co. Durham, England, Bowes Mus.

St. Anthony of Padua, 1659
Madrid, School of Agriculture

The Assumption, 1666
Leningrad, Hermitage

The Transfiguration
Barcelona, Mus. of Art

See also page 268

PEDRO DE CAMPAÑA

1503 - about 1580

A Fleming who became one of the early masters of Spanish painting

Pedro de Campaña was born into an illustrious Brussels family in 1503. Pedro de Campaña is the Castilian form of his real name, which was Pieter Kempeneer. His early education was probably Italian, since he worked in Bologna in 1529 on decorations to celebrate Emperor Charles V's entry into the city. Afterwards, he went to Venice, and from 1537 on he was in Seville. Campaña must have married Beatriz de Seguera soon after reaching Seville, as one of his daughters was married in 1556.

Campaña enjoyed a great reputation and the friendship both of aristocrats, such as the Dukes of Alcalá, and of his colleagues, such as Francisco Pacheco, who

St. Anthony and St. Paul (detail)
Seville, S. Isidro

painted a portrait of him. In 1563 he left Seville and returned to the Netherlands. He was made chief of a tapestry-making concern in Brussels, for which he prepared cartoons until 1580. He is presumed to have died in that year.

The strong personality of Pedro de Campaña—a Fleming well acquainted with Italian art—soon made itself felt in Seville, at that time a city rich in wealth and in patrons of the arts. His first known work is *The Deposition*, 1540, which seems to have been inspired by the well-known print by Marcantonio Raimondi and painted for the Church of S. María de Gracia. The success of this composition perhaps brought the commission in 1546 for another *Deposition*, this time for Seville Cathedral. The contract specified that it should be "as good as, or even better than" the first. Campaña lived up to the contract, and his real reputation was founded by this painting.

G. Kubler and M. Soria   Art and Architecture in Spain and Portugal   London, 1959

Sacrifice of Callirrhoë (detail)
Madrid, Real Acad. de San Fernando

DAMIÁN CAMPENY
1771-1855

One of the most notable of the Neoclassic Spanish sculptors

Damián Buenaventura Campeny y Estrany, son of Andrés Campeny and Casilda Estrany, was born in Mataró, Barcelona province, on April 12, 1771. He started his training making clay models. As a result, a priest, Don José Camín, arranged for the boy to help the sculptor Salvador Gurri. In 1778 Gurri took Campeny to the city of Barcelona to study at the Chamber of Commerce. In 1796 he competed for a grant for study in Rome, won it, and at the same time received another from Charles IV. He stayed in Rome, where he became the friend of Antonio Canova, until 1816, returning to Barcelona on January 4th of that year.

In 1818 he married Mariana Gassol, and on February 3, 1820, he was elected to the Academy of San Fernando. In 1825 he agreed with the Chamber of Commerce to make one sculpture a year in exchange for a position, but in 1844 he had a legal quarrel with that body. The following year he was appointed member of the Academy of San Luis, at Saragossa.

Campeny's *Dead Lucretia* achieved fame from an unusual source. As soon as it became known in Barcelona, the sculptor was accused of having imitated an ancient work. To some extent, Campeny lacked originality, for he had produced a Neoclassical-type statue common through Europe, that of the seated Roman woman. Nevertheless, *The Dead Lucretia* is an intrinsically beautiful piece, and it is executed in marble with an unusual virtuosity. Campeny died in San Gervasio, Barcelona, on July 7, 1855.

ALONSO CANO

A Baroque painter, architect, and sculptor

Alonso Cano was born in Granada on March 19, 1601, the contemporary of Francisco de Zurbarán and Diego Velázquez. Both his parents came originally from the Don Quixote country of La Mancha. His father, Miguel Cano, was an architect and builder of altarpiece settings, and it was probably he who gave his son his first grounding in architecture and the appreciation of painting. When Alonso was 13, Juan del Castillo, later the teacher of Bartolomé Murillo, came to Granada on a visit. He saw the boy's work and advised his father to take him to Seville, into an artistic atmosphere suitable to his talents. The family moved, and at 15 Cano was apprenticed, as Velázquez was, to Francisco Pacheco. Later he had lessons from Castillo, and studied Roman sculpture from the statues in the Seville palace of the duke of Alcalá. His education was broad enough to allow him to do the architectural design and the sculpture as well as the painting of his altarpieces.

It was perhaps this very diffusion of energy that in the end vitiated Cano's painting. Within ten years he was a known and established master of brilliantly simple forms, emphasized, sometimes idealized, by their pure outlines and thrusts of shadow-producing light. He was admired by the young Murillo, and indebted in his turn to the work of his friend Velázquez. When Zurbarán moved to Seville in 1628, he also benefited from Cano's influence.

Cano, however, failed to mature on the lines of his early promise. He was a vain, quarrelsome, adventurous man, and he began to envy Zurbarán's new reputation in Seville. When Zurbarán's name was proposed for the office of painter to the city, Cano organized a petition of Seville artists to protest. In 1638 he provoked another

Self-portrait (detail)
Cadiz, Provincial Mus.

One of the Gothic Kings for the Palace of Madrid   *Madrid, Prado*

Two of the Gothic Kings for the Palace of Madrid
Madrid, Prado

St. Agnes
East Berlin, Staatl. Mus.

HIS WORKS INCLUDE

The Madonna and Child, 1629-31
Lebrija, S. Maria
The Angel and St. John the Evangelist
1635-37
London, Wallace Coll.
The Descent into Limbo,
about 1637-40
Los Angeles, Calif., County Mus.

See also pages 245, 266, 267, 284

artist to a duel. Cano left him wounded and had to flee to Madrid. Velázquez, who had lived there for 15 years, found him a patron, the Count-Duke Olivares, and a job as drawing master to the Infante Balthasar Carlos.

Two years later a fire in the palace damaged the king's pictures, and Cano was asked to restore paintings by Rubens and Titian. He took the opportunity to study the whole collection of Flemish and Italian works. This contact with the great Venetian colorists, as well as his personal experience of Velázquez at work, animating every object with silvery high-lights, made his coloring deeper and more confident, his compositions less strict, and his sacred subjects earthier. Human figures, like the portraits of the Gothic kings commissioned in 1643, began to look gentle, even approachable.

This period in the early 1640's was the calmest period of Cano's life. It was broken in 1644 by the death of his wife. He was charged with murder, but escaped and took refuge, first in Valencia, and then in other towns and villages, sometimes very near Madrid. He returned to Madrid only a year later in 1645. Within four years he was fully reinstated at court, and in 1652 he was appointed prebendary of Granada Cathedral.

Cano thus returned to his birthplace, where he began his most important paintings, a series of seven huge canvases, *The Seven Joys of Mary*, for the cathedral. His inspiration was more Baroque, more emotional, and grander than before, but also more erratic. His work was interrupted by quarrels with the cathedral canons, who succeeded in 1656 in having him removed. Cano afterwards lived in Madrid until 1660 when the king restored him to the cathedral. There he continued and finished, in 1664, *The Seven Joys of Mary*, whose dramatic, understandable style drew some followers and made him the founder of the School of Granada.

H. Wethey   Alonso Cano   Cambridge, Mass., 1955

St. Juan Capistrano and St. Bernardine of Siena, 1653-57
Granada, Provincial Mus.

St. John the Evangelist (detail)
Budapest, Mus. of Fine Arts

JUAN CARREÑO DE MIRANDA 1614-1685

The greatest fresco painter of the Madrid School

Juan Carreño de Miranda was born in Avilés, Asturias, on March 25, 1614, the son of Juan Carreño and Catalina Fernández Bermúdez. His stay in Asturias was a short one, as he began learning his profession in Valladolid while still a child. He studied there with two painters—his uncle Andrés Carreño de Miranda, and Diego Valentín Díaz, the greatest painter of Valladolid. Carreño then went to Madrid to continue his apprenticeship under Pedro de las Cuevas and Bartolomé Román. Soon he received important commissions, like that of 1634 for the decoration of the cloister of the College of Doña María de Aragón. He married María de Medina. In 1669 he was appointed painter to the king and, two years later, to the royal chamber, painting no less than 17 royal portraits.

Among his contemporaries Carreño enjoyed the reputation of a kind and simple man without a trace of the hauteur that his position as the greatest fresco painter of the Madrid School might well have permitted him. Ironically, Carreño was better known for his many monotonous portraits of King Charles II and his mother, Mariana of Austria, than he was for his frescoes. His style of portrait painting followed the great tradition of Velázquez, while the obvious influence of Sir Anthony van Dyck is seen in his religious paintings.

Apart from his royal portraits, Carreño created other notable compositions, such as the religious painting, *The Baptism of Christ*, about 1682, inspired by Jacopo Tintoretto. Almost all his paintings are of the highest quality and justify the title of successor to Velázquez that was Carreño's until his death in Madrid, October 3, 1685.

E. Harris Spanish Painting London, 1938

The Ambassador Potemkin, 1681
Madrid, Prado

HIS WORKS INCLUDE

The Founding of the Trinitarian Order, 1666 *Paris, Louvre*

The Immaculate Conception, 1670 *New York, Hispanic Society*

The Duke of Pastrana, about 1680 *Madrid, Prado*

See also page 270

JAIME CASTAYLS died 1377

A 14th-century sculptor of Catalan altarpieces

Little is known of Jaime Castayls' early life, apart from the fact that he was born in Berga, Lérida province, in the 14th century and that he married a daughter of the painter Ferrer Bassa. In 1345 he completed an altarpiece for Cornellá de Conflent in the eastern Pyrenees, a work of art both delicate and complex. From 1349 he worked in company with Master Aloy on the royal tombs and altarpieces in the monastery church of Poblet in Tarragona. From 1360 Castayls was occupied as the chief craftsman on the art works of Lérida Cathedral, where he was certainly still employed ten years later. At the same time he continued with the Poblet commission, finishing it in 1377.

The complex aesthetic style of Castayls shares elements from the schools of Gerona and Lérida but, at the same time, shows definite Italian influence along

St. Charlemagne (detail) 14th century
Gerona, Cath.

with certain archaisms. His most perfect and original sculpture is the altarpiece of Cornellá de Conflent, which is a typical example of Catalan altarpieces of the 14th century in its oblong form with The Virgin in the center. When assessing his work at Poblet, allowance must be made for the somewhat repetitive character of this collection, the fact that many helpers shared the work, and that when it was being executed Castayls was also working on Lérida Cathedral.

The Martyrdom of St. Pelayo (detail)
1645   *Cordova, Cath.*

ANTONIO DEL CASTILLO   1616-1668

A leading Baroque painter and draftsman of Cordova

Antonio del Castillo was born in 1616 in Cordova. He studied with his father Agustín del Castillo and his uncle Juan del Castillo (the pupil of Francisco de Zurbarán and the teacher of Bartolomé Murillo).

St. John the Baptist, about 1635, is one of Castillo's earliest paintings. The vegetation and landscape were derived from the same Flemish engravings by Marten de Vos that had influenced Zurbarán and Sebastián de Herrera Barnuevo. However, the facial type and modeling of drapery recall the artistic style of Juan del Castillo. In the 1640's Castillo began introducing vivid action in background groups, as seen in the Baroque *The Martyrdom of St. Pelayo*, 1645. About this time, Castillo saw Zurbarán's paintings (now lost) in the Church of S. Pablo at Cordova, and a new largeness of form was suggested to him. His powerful *S. Bonaventura* is an example of Zurbaránesque style.

During the 1650's, Castillo began to copy engravings by the Hollander Abraham Bloemaert. Castillo's penmanship, composition, and facial types emulated Bloemaert. He filled his sketchbook with charming heads and Dutch pastoral scenes. Castillo's finest work, obviously influenced by the Netherlandish style, was six scenes from the life of Joseph. They combined picturesque grandeur, firm design, sweeping compositions, airiness, and varied lighting. They showed that Castillo was capable of vehemence as well as being a highly proficient draftsman.

The Triumph of Pharaoh of Egypt
(detail) 1655   *Madrid, Prado*

CLAUDIO COELLO

about 1642-1693

The last Spanish master of the Madrid School

Claudio Coello was born in Madrid to a Spanish mother and a Portuguese father, Faustino Coello, a bronzeworker. His father placed him in the house of Francisco Rizi, a dramatically Baroque painter, to learn metal chasing, intending him to to help in the family workshop. But Rizi saw the direction of the boy's talent, and persuaded his father to let him be a painter. Coello worked night and day at Rizi's until he was far ahead of the other students, and sometimes was allowed to collaborate with his master. At 21, while still Rizi's pupil, he had his first success, a large, blatantly brilliant painting for the high altar of the Benedictine Convent of S. Plácido in Madrid. Another picture of the same date was so much to Rizi's taste that he offered permission for it to be shown as his own so that Coello might get more money for it. But the artist preferred to enjoy his *succès d'estime*.

Juan Carreño de Miranda was a friend of Rizi. Once Velázquez's assistant, Carreño had become a painter at the Spanish court. He too became the teacher and friend of Coello, giving him the opportunity to make many copies of pictures by Titian, Rubens, and van Dyck, among others in the palace collections. Another friend was José Jiménez Donoso, just back from Rome and beginning to take up his contacts again in Madrid. He arranged a succession of commissions for frescoes for Coello, collaborating on some of them himself. One was designs for the entry into Madrid of Queen Maria Luisa of Bourbon, on her marriage to Charles II of Spain. In 1671 the two artists painted frescoes in Toledo Cathedral. In 1683, Coello spent a year in Saragossa on frescoes ordered by the archbishop for the Augustinian Convent of La Manteria.

Self-portrait (detail)
Madrid, National Palace

Jesus as a Child in the Door of the Temple   *Madrid, Prado*

St. Catherine of Alexandria
London, Apsley House

The Triumph of St. Augustine, 1664
Madrid, Prado

173

Portrait of Charles II
Madrid, Prado

HIS WORKS INCLUDE

The Madonna Adored by St. Louis
of France, 1669
Madrid, Prado

The Adoration of the Sacred
Host, 1685-90
near Madrid, The Escorial, Monastery

S. Tomas de Villanueva, 1692
Salamanca, El Carmin de Abajo

See also pages 249, 270, 271

Back in Madrid at the beginning of 1684, Coello was made honorary painter to the king. As a result of Rizi's death in 1685, Coello had to paint almost the whole of a huge canvas, *The Adoration of the Sacred Host*, that Rizi had started for the sacristy altar of the Escorial. The project involved portraits of all the nobles at court, of King Charles, and of Coello himself. When the king had granted the necessary sittings, an attendant count pointed out that here was the new court painter.

The preliminary sketches for *The Adoration of the Sacred Host*, which Coello had decided to repaint entirely, kept him in residence at the Escorial for another four years. In 1690 the final painting was done. It was the culminating achievement of a talent at ease only in huge complicated compositions, where a masterly sense of balance, space, and movement might show itself to advantage. Details, like the portraits, were alive and full of character in the tradition of Velázquez. The picture was admired by the king and court.

The sensitivity which had attracted both friends and collaborators also made Coello susceptible to insult, whether real or imagined. When in 1692 the king invited an Italian, the swift, spectacular painter Luca Giordano, to come to Madrid and fresco the ceilings of the Escorial, Coello (though still esteemed by the whole court, and by Giordano himself) refused to paint again. Coello's chronic respiratory weakness became aggravated, and he died on April 20, 1693, in Madrid.

A. de Beruete y Moret   The School of Madrid   London and New York, 1911

The Madonna of the Councilors
(detail) 1443-45
Barcelona, Mus. of Art

LUIS DALMÁU   died about 1460

A painter of Valencia and Barcelona who worked almost exclusively in the Flemish style

Luis Dalmáu was born probably in Valencia. In 1428 as a practicing master in that town, he was appointed court painter to the king of Aragón, Alfonso V. Next year his traveling expenses were paid as a member of a mission sent to Castile to find a wife for the king's brother.

Meanwhile, Dalmáu had met the Flemish master Jan van Eyck. The latter was court painter to Philip the Good, duke of Burgundy, and he made two journeys to Spain and Portugal on secret missions to arrange a marriage for the duke. At Valencia in 1427, van Eyck painted a portrait of one prospective wife, Isabel de Urgel. Dalmáu was so impressed that he persuaded the king of Aragón to send him to Flanders. The Spanish painter set out in 1431. In van Eyck's studio in Bruges the altarpiece begun in 1427 for St. Bavon Cathedral in Ghent was then nearing completion, and Dalmáu apprenticed himself to van Eyck.

Five years later he was back in Valencia, but by 1443, after a short time in Aragón, he was settled in Barcelona, where he resided until his death some 20 years later. It was probably the commission for the altarpiece of *The Madonna of the*

Councilors, his greatest work, that attracted him there. The five town councilors of 1443 had decided to improve their chapel with a splendid altarpiece, for which they wished to obtain "the best and most suitable painter that can be found." Within two months they had engaged Dalmáu. He was not wealthy at the time, and was forced to use yellow paint for the border of the Madonna's mantle, not the gold that the councilors had specified. Later, in 1460, he was employed by the new king of Aragón, Juan II, and asked to decorate the tomb of his old master, Alfonso V. Soon afterwards Dalmáu died, possibly from the plague that broke out in Barcelona about this time.

Dalmáu had escaped the Valencia tradition, in which he had been brought up, of painting only grand single figures on plain backgrounds of gold. Instead he copied quite uncritically from his master van Eyck. The composition of the altarpiece of the councilors is derived closely from van Eyck's Ghent altarpiece. The backgrounds are landscape, the portraits of the councilors are three-quarter face, and the singing angels are placed in tight groups. The types, too, are van Eyck's; St. Andrew's hairy head is a replica of that of St. John the Baptist from the Ghent work.

C. Zervos *Catalan Art* London, *1937*
C. R. Post *A History of Spanish Painting, Vols. VI, VII* Cambridge, Mass., *1930-58*

Angel of the Annunciation (detail)
Valencia, Mus. de B. A.

HIS WORKS INCLUDE
The Annunciation
Valencia, Mus. de B. A.

See also page 219

JERÓNIMO JACINTO DE ESPINOSA   1600-1667

A 17th-century painter of religious subjects

Jerónimo Jacinto de Espinosa was born on July 16, 1600, in Cocentina, Valencia province. His father, Jerónimo Rodríguez de Espinosa, was his first teacher. In 1616 he registered for an examination to qualify as a master of the painters' guild. After spending three more years in his father's workshop, Espinosa passed the examination in 1619. He married Doña Jerónima de Castro on April 2, 1622.

The subjects of Espinosa's numerous works are all religious. The *Portrait of the Dominican Monk Gerónimo Mos*, about 1625-28, is one of the most psychologically intense studies of a Spanish monk in the 17th century, comparable only to those of Zurbarán. *The Death of St. Luis Beltran*, 1653, is an enormous and typically Baroque composition in the style of El Greco's *Burial of Count Orgaz*, that is to say, with

The Holy Family, 1658
Valencia, Mus. de B. A.

the lower half strongly realistic and the upper part showing supernatural manifestations. The final masterpiece by Espinosa is *The Last Communion of St. Mary Magdalen*, 1665, a perfect harmony of composition, drawing, light, and color. He continued as the favorite painter for the monasteries and religious orders of Valencia until his death.

Espinosa was one of those painters who developed his first ideas for paintings in truly masterly sketches, usually very simple in form and skillfully shaded. A sketch normally contained only one of the figures that were later to make up the complete picture. Espinosa died in Valencia in 1667, too close to religious life to have become a popular painter.

G. Kubler and M. Soria   Art and Architecture in Spain and Portugal   London, 1959

St. Francis Xavier (detail)
Valladolid, S. Miguel

GREGORIO FERNÁNDEZ   about 1576-1636

A Spanish sculptor known for the nobility of his dramatic expression

Gregorio Fernández was born somewhere in Galicia, possibly at Sarria (Lugo province), which he mentions in his will. His date of birth is probably 1576, as Fernández himself in 1610 said that he was 34. He moved to Valladolid at an early age and became the pupil of the obscure sculptor Francisco del Rincón. About 1603 he married María Pérez, who bore him two sons. Fernández lived a life of intense and quiet dedication to his work, in a family atmosphere of piety and charity toward the poor. A portrait painted by Diego Valentín Díaz, the most important painter in Valladolid at that time, shows Fernández to be dark with an intelligent forehead, large eyes, ugly nose, moustache, and small goatee beard.

His first known work is *Christ Recumbent*, which, according to tradition, was commissioned personally by King Philip III in the days when Valladolid was the capital of Spain. This work was a success, not only in its dramatic expression, but also in its very precise study of nudity. In fact, the success was so great that it gave rise to a large number of later variations, and Fernández himself made another version, almost as beautiful as the original, for the Benedictine Convent of S. Plácido in Madrid. Also of great merit is his *Pietà*, completed in 1617 for the Church of Las Angustias in Valladolid. It is a perfectly harmonious work, with a strong diagonal form, the only Baroque element found in his *oeuvre*. Fernández usually demonstrated an almost classical restraint and serenity, very different from the agitated movement that Alonso Berruguete and Juan de Juni had given to the sculpture of Valladolid. Fernández fell ill on Christmas Day, 1635, and died in Valladolid on January 22, 1636.

G. Kubler and M. Soria   Art and Architecture in Spain and Portugal   London, 1959

FERNANDO GALLEGO   between 1440 and 1445 - after 1507

The most influential master of the early Castilian School

Apart from his own pupils, Fernando Gallego was almost the only painter of his time in the Castilian provinces of Salamanca and Zamora. Yet scarcely anything is known about his life. He was born at Salamanca, and traveled about Castile, executing a great many commissions in different parts of the region. Just before 1467 his earliest known work, *The St. Ildefonso Altarpiece*, was ordered by Cardinal Juan de Mella for Zamora Cathedral. In 1468 he was painting for Palencia Cathedral, with such success that five years later he was asked to undertake no less than six altars for Coria Cathedral nearby. In 1507 he was painting both the gallery of the university chapel in his home town, and an altarpiece for the old cathedral there. This was the last record of him, but he is said to have lived to an advanced age.

During Gallego's lifetime large numbers of prints made by his contemporary, the German artist Martin Schongauer, were being sold regularly in the fairs of Castile. Most of the Castilian painting of the period was influenced by them, and Gallego's work from first to last was no exception. For example, he certainly saw Schongauer's series of engravings of *The Passion*, before he began the Crucifixion panel in his *St. Ildefonso Altarpiece*, and had these still in mind at the time of painting his altarpiece for the Old Cathedral of Salamanca in 1507.

Certain indications, like the flying scrolls of *The St. Ildefonso Altarpiece*, suggest that Gallego had also seen Flemish pictures or prints. There are reflections in his work of the emotional content of Dieric Bouts and Roger van der Weyden. The style of these Flemish painters, however, was no more than the basis of Gallego's own style which was strong, unstereotyped, and so realistic that it sometimes produced strange melodramatic distortions—twisted garments or poses, protruding eyes, and mobile lips. Such distortions were a peculiarly Spanish phenomenon that had appeared 50 years before in the work of Luis Borrassá, and in Ferrer Bassa's work 50 years before that. Gallego's simplified textures and smooth surfaces,

The St. Ildefonso Altarpiece (detail) about 1467
Zamora, Cath.

177

whether of brocade or grass, confirm this preoccupation not with the merely decorative but with forms themselves.

Gallego had pupils and imitators in many parts of Spain, even as far south as Estremadura and the frontiers of Portugal. More important, the young Pedro Berruguete was brought up near Palencia and probably went to Gallego to learn the appreciation and practice of Flemish techniques.

C. R. Post   A History of Spanish Painting, Vols. IV, V   Cambridge, Mass., 1930-58

Calvary, before 1467
Madrid, Prado

Pietà, before 1467
Madrid, Prado

FRANCISCO DE GOYA Y LUCIENTES   1746-1828

A great genius, versatile and inexhaustible

Francisco de Goya y Lucientes was born on March 30, 1746 in Fuendetodos, a small, poor village on the dry plain of Aragón, where his mother Doña Gracia Lucientes was staying in the house of her aristocratic relations. Later they went to join his father, Francisco de Paula José Goya, a gilder in Saragossa. Goya went to a monastery school, then to drawing class, and finally at 14 he spent four years in the studio workshop of José Luzan. His master was not a painter of note and it was probably Goya's home background and his firsthand experience of a craftsman at work which gave him his pertinacious artistic ambitions. He went twice to Madrid; at 17 when he was still an apprentice, and at 20, to try, and fail, the competitions for entrance to the Real Academia de San Fernando. On the second occasion he probably took lessons from Francisco Bayeu, a Saragossan 12 years his senior whom he had known at Luzan's. But Bayeu's art, like Luzan's, lacked vitality, and three years later Goya made a working trip to Italy. He visited Rome and in a competition at the Royal Academy of Fine Arts at Parma in 1770 he was congratulated by the jury on his painting of *Hannibal Crossing the Alps*.

When Goya returned home in 1771, probably through France, he was more successful. He immediately received some small orders in Saragossa, including one for frescoes for the cathedral vault. About two years later he was able to settle in Madrid, where he collaborated with his former teacher, Bayeu. In 1773, he married Bayeu's sister, Josefa. In 1774 the German Neoclassic artist Anton Raphael Mengs was on his second visit to the Spanish court, where he was Bayeu's superior in the work of decorating the royal palaces. He sent for Goya with an invitation to become a tapestry designer at the Royal Workshop of St. Barbara. In 1775 Goya began the first of 60 tapestry cartoons, which occupied much of his attention until 1792. Under such titles as *The Sunshade*, *The Washerwomen*, *The Crockery Vendor*, they portrayed various aspects of Madrid life, and indicated his progress from the mismanagement of an apparently unwieldy medium to an easy mastery of his themes and techniques. This period, which lasted until he was 46 and might have contained the whole *oeuvre* of a less persistent genius, turned out to be merely the foundation of what was to come. Goya lived to be 82, and these profitable years of self-education were perhaps a compensation for his inadequate early training.

The most striking characteristics of his cartoons were their light, uncomplicated

Self-portrait, about 1816
Madrid, Prado

The Clothed Maja (detail) about 1799
Madrid, Prado

Que tal? (Old Woman)
Lille, France, Palais des B-A.

touch and coloring, but even while making them Goya took his artistic development seriously. Granted permission in 1778 to visit the palace collections of Italian, Flemish, and Spanish paintings, he made his first devoted study of the great masters. He executed 18 etchings of canvases by Velázquez, among them the multiple portrait composition, *The Maids of Honor*. Goya's own first dated portrait had been painted in 1774, but others followed only desultorily. Then, in 1787, he was appointed one of the king's painters. Other appointments followed, and with them a long series of portraits.

Goya became court painter at the accession of Charles IV in 1789. To the end of his life, he produced portraits ranging from aristocrats and their children, the king and queen, the great actors, actresses, toreadors, politicians, and generals of the day, to the later, quieter portraits of his grandchild. The composition of *The Family of Charles IV*, 1800, with Goya himself at work in the background, was inspired by Velázquez's *The Maids of Honor*. Throughout Goya's life, he also produced portraits of his own close friends: statesmen, poets, writers, and painters, both enlightened liberals and conservative academicians.

Goya did not allow the empty contemporary academism to obstruct his individuality. He was elected in 1780 to the Real Academia de San Fernando, and like Bayeu and other academicians, Goya was commissioned by the king to produce one of seven conventional altar paintings for the Madrid Church of S. Fernando el Grande. He executed a *St. Bernardine of Siena Preaching in the Presence of Alfonso V*, which at the unveiling in 1784 was judged the best. The next year he was made

Don Manuel Osorio de Zuñiga, 1784
New York, Met. Mus., Jules S. Bache Coll.

Majas on a Balcony (detail) 1810-15
New York, Met. Mus., H. O. Havemeyer Coll.

deputy director of painting at the academy. Goya's appointments at court provided him with generous stipends. In 1792 he went to stay at Cadiz with his friend Sebastián Martinéz. A portrait of Martinéz marked Goya's rejection of bright colors in favor of the silver grays, which he used in future portraits to express subtly the lightness of drapery over the substantial volumes of a body.

In 1792 Goya fell desperately ill, and when after several months he recovered, he was permanently deaf. The pain that he endured caused a rebirth, a self-revaluation. In fact, he began to paint largely for himself. With the addition of some blacks and browns and touches of a dull pink, or raw red or ocher, the neutral palette which he had adopted in 1792 perfectly served the nightmarish "fancy and invention" (his own words) which accompanied the terrible intermittent noises produced inside his head by deafness. His subjects, in such pictures as *The Madhouse*, or *The Burial of the Sardine*, were human beings, or witches, in the grip of overwhelming emotions. There was a touch of satire made possible only by his new independence of the human race.

On Bayeu's death in 1795, Goya became director of painting at the academy, but he resigned after two years. He was dependent on no one, except perhaps the beautiful, frivolous duchess of Alba. He painted her portrait in 1795, and again in 1797 when she was a widow. He traveled with her to her Andalusian estate in Sanlúcar. She appeared many times in Goya's work before she died in 1802. Her exact role in his life and her importance to him has been the subject of much conjecture, ranging from the over-sentimental to the absolutely dismissive.

Goya's art had already reached its peak of detachment in a book of 82 etchings published in 1799, *The Caprices*, an exemplar of the petty stupidities of men and women. They feature a realism combined with a new fantastic imagery of witches, hags, and donkeys, and a brilliant exploitation of *chiaroscuro* in the tradition of his model, Rembrandt.

The second great crisis of Goya's life was the occupation of Spain by Napoleon,

The Firing Squad (detail): from The Disasters of War, 1810-13 (etching) *Madrid, Real Acad. de San Fernando, et al.*

Total War (detail): from The Disasters of War, 1810-13 (etching) *Madrid, Real Acad. de San Fernando, et al.*

The Second of May, after 1814 *Madrid, Prado*

the popular war of independence that started in Madrid on May 2, 1808, and the fall of the monarchy. Though revolted by the chaos and bloodshed, he stayed in Madrid, made many paintings and drawings of catastrophe, and another etched series, *The Disasters of War*, 1810-13. These etchings were not made public during Goya's lifetime. The majority recorded episodes of the Napoleonic war in Spain; the rest are allegories of man's brutality in a political situation.

The monarchy was restored in 1814 and largely supplanted, but not actually dethroned, by the liberals in 1820, the year in which Goya swore enthusiastic allegiance to the liberal constitution. In 1819 Goya suffered another spell of illness which prompted from the old unbeliever two somber pictures full of religious awe. He had by this time made his first lithographs and, from 1820, worked on his last etchings. These were his supreme achievements in this medium, the obscure, savage *Follies*. During this period he painted onto the walls of his new house his darkest, most horrifying dream of all, the 14 *Black Paintings*, 1820-22.

In 1823 Goya was 77. There were reprisals against the liberals, and, leaving his house to his 17-year-old grandson Mariano, Goya went into hiding. In the next year, with permission from the king, whose first court painter he still was, he went to France. He spent July and August in Paris, then settled in Bordeaux with his mistress Rosario Leocadia Weiss and her two children, and continued to paint and draw. Goya returned to Madrid only on short working visits before he died in Bordeaux on April 16, 1828.

One of Goya's last drawings was called *I Am Still Learning*, and a year before he died he produced something entirely new, *The Milkmaid of Bordeaux*. This, one of the first intimations of Impressionism, was created with a delicate virtuosity out of sudden bursts of light and greenish and bluish glints.

X. de Salas   The Drawings and Lithographs of Goya   London, 1954
E. du G. Trapier   Goya: A Study of His Portraits, 1797-99   New York, 1955
E. Lafuente Ferrari   The Graphic Works of Goya   London, 1962
S. Cantosi   The Life and Works of Goya   Madrid, 1964

Witches' Sabbath, 1820-22
Madrid, Prado

EL GRECO

A cosmopolitan genius, painter, architect, and sculptor who produced a fervent and original art

El Greco was born Domenikos Theotokopoulos in Crete, probably in or near Candia, of a prosperous Greek family. As Crete was a Venetian possession at the time of his birth, about 1541, he received an education on the new broad lines of Italian humanism that gave him a lifelong interest in almost every subject. In his library at his death there were the works of Greek, Latin, and Italian poets, orators, philosophers, and storytellers, as well as spiritual, historical, and even medical works. El Greco himself had a reputation as a scholar, and wrote on painting, sculpture, and at length on architecture.

Portrait of an Unknown Man (believed to be a self-portrait) about 1600
Madrid, Prado

For his first painting lessons the young Cretan went to the local monks, who taught him to make icons in the flat, mystical manner they had inherited from Byzantium. This mysticism remained the basis of his style, even though at about 19 he went abroad to finish his training and underwent a series of quite different influences. He never returned to his native island.

It was natural that El Greco should go first to Venice, where there was a large and respected Greek colony. According to some modern writers, El Greco was already a master painter when he arrived in Venice. Nevertheless, he apprenticed himself to the greatest Italian painters of the day, first in the studio of Jacopo Bassano, and then in 1565-66 in that of Tintoretto. He made such progress that he was accepted in 1567 as the pupil of the greatest of all Venetian painters, Titian. He benefited less from him, however, than he had from Tintoretto, who first revealed to El Greco the pictorial force of strong movement, and the technique of expressing it. From Tintoretto he also learned the usefulness of making little wax, wood, or clay figures as models to be moved, grouped, and painted from unusual, often foreshortened, angles. In Rome, where he went in 1569, El Greco absorbed the emotional, idealizing elongations and distortions of central Italian Mannerism.

Knight with his Hand on his Breast (detail) about 1583
Madrid, Prado

The thriving posthumous influence of Michelangelo stimulated his genius, already half-formed on Mannerist lines by Tintoretto. Before he had been in Rome three years, he was heard to say that he could make a new *Last Judgment* for the Sistine Chapel as good as Michelangelo's, and with the figures properly clothed. This was not so much an idle boast as a statement of his feeling that he could equal the master, whose flocks of unquestioning imitators made life in Rome so impossible for him that in 1572 he left the city and the circle of painters, writers, and scholars whom he had made his friends. One or two of them were Spaniards, and it was perhaps their reminiscences that prompted him to sail for Spain. Five years later he was established in Toledo with an excellent reputation as an artist, so much so that he received an important commission to paint eight pictures for the altar of the Old Convent Church of the Order of San Domingo (Bernardines).

St. Jerome as a Cardinal, about 1600
London, N. G.

The following year, 1578, his son Jorge Manuel, eventually a painter, sculptor, and architect, was born. Jorge's mother was the beautiful Toledan woman Doña Jerónima de las Cuevas with whom El Greco stayed in Toledo for the rest of his life. He still did not speak Spanish, only Italian and Greek (he never signed his

View of Toledo, 1604-14
New York, Met. Mus.,
H. O. Havemayer Coll.

pictures with any but his original Greek name), but the cosmopolitan atmosphere of Toledo as a European center for trade, religion, scholarship, and the arts would have made any foreigner feel at home. Its ready welcome and appreciation of the painter were reflected in commissions that poured in from its churches and convents, the learned gatherings to which he was invited, and the friendships he formed with men of every distinction—poets, writers, lawyers, and even explorers.

This pleasant existence was broken only once or twice in the 36 years El Greco lived in Toledo. Once, his *Espolio*, 1579, was refused by the cathedral chapter for whom it was painted on the grounds that it was too loud, and too unconventionally characterized; it now hangs in the cathedral sacristy. *The Martyrdom of St. Maurice and the Theban Legion*, 1580-82, commissioned by King Philip II as a test case, appalled the king for much the same reasons. Philip objected to its lack of devotional coloring and its cavalier treatment of the sacred theme—the martyrdom of the 40,000—which was relegated to the background. Nevertheless, Philip II kept the painting in his great collection at the Escorial.

This setback destroyed El Greco's chance of a secure post at court, but did not alter his reputation in Spain generally. Nor was his idea of the unique position of the artist in society dislodged by his own misfortune. He was prepared to go to law in defense of the exemption of works of art from taxes, and from 1605 to 1607 he argued precisely this point in a suit against the tax collector of Illescas. In fact, his

The Martyrdom of St. Maurice and the
Theban Legion, 1580-82
near Madrid, The Escorial

St. Martin and the Beggar, 1597-99
Washington, D. C., N. G., Widener Coll.

The Holy Trinity, 1577-79
Madrid, Prado

184

reaction at court set him firmly on the path of his own individual or, as it was then construed, eccentric art.

El Greco had now achieved the full integration of Byzantine with Venetian and Roman painting. To carry out his swirling Mannerist compositions he continued to make little figurines to use as models. He was also a sculptor in his own right, making statues, or designs for statues, for churches in Toledo and other towns. His painting retained its Italian qualities of massive relief and energetic movement, qualities further supplemented by his instinctive feeling for the real and the tangible that he assimilated in Spain. An equally traditional Spanish spirituality also took root in his emotionally heightened genius. To its service he brought Mannerist forms, figures too tall to be natural—they have sometimes been ascribed to madness or defective eyesight—but effectively expressing the ideal. Most characteristic of all was his mastery of rushing color, bursts of light, and the specks of highlighting that inspired Velázquez and forecast much of modern painting.

As long as El Greco could paint at full capacity, he prospered to the extent of being able to afford a luxurious suite of 24 rooms with gardens at the Marquis de Villena's palace. But toward the end of his life his health declined, and when Velázquez's teacher, Francisco Pacheco, came from Seville to visit him in 1611, El Greco could not walk with his guest to his own studio. This incapacity, combined with expensive standards of living, left him sometimes in financial difficulties. At times he sent his pictures to be sold in Seville for shipping to the West Indies and America. He died, on April 7, 1614, in Toledo. His friends, the poet Luis de Gongora y Argote and the Jesuit Paravicino, together wrote three sonnets on his death.

E. du G. Trapier El Greco's Early Years at Toledo, 1576-86 New York, 1958
P. Keleman El Greco Revisited New York, 1961
H. E. Wethey El Greco and His School Princeton, N. J., 1962

HIS WORKS INCLUDE

Vincentio Anastagi, 1570?
New York, Frick Coll.

The Assumption, 1577
Chicago, Art Inst.

The Agony in the Garden,
about 1580-86
Toledo, Ohio, Art Mus.

St. Louis of France, about 1570
Paris, Louvre

The Baptism of Christ
about 1595-1600
Madrid, Prado

The Resurrection, 1608-10
Madrid, Prado

The Visitation, about 1610
Washington, D. C., N. G.

The Vision of the Apocalypse,
about 1610
New York, Met. Mus.

See also pages 229, 230, 231, 232, 233, 260, 281

Christ Driving the Traders from the Temple, about 1595
London, N. G.

Laocoön, about 1610-14
Washington, D. C., N. G., Kress Coll.

Chorus of Angels
London, B. M.

HIS WORKS INCLUDE

Ecstasy of St. Augustine, about 1670
Madrid, S. Francisco el Grande

St. Barnabas
near Madrid, The Escorial

St. Joseph
New York, Hispanic Society

See also page 269

SEBASTIÁN DE HERRERA BARNUEVO   1619-1671

An outstanding figure in the history of the art of Madrid

Sebastián de Herrera Barnuevo was born in Madrid in 1619, son of the sculptor Antonio de Herrera Barnuevo and of Sebastiana Sanchez. He was instructed by his father until Alonso Cano's arrival in Madrid in 1638, when the youth was attracted by the strong personality of the artist from Granada. The first important known work of Herrera was his share in the decorations to celebrate the entrance of the queen, Mariana of Austria, into the city on November 15, 1649. For this and similar tasks, Herrera was rewarded with the position of valet by Philip IV. On February 26, 1662, he obtained the post of chief architect of royal building projects. On November 26, 1668, he was appointed court painter, and in 1670 he was named keeper of the Escorial. Herrera died in Madrid at the beginning of 1671.

Unfortunately, almost all Herrera's paintings have disappeared. He had a share in decorations for the Chapel of S. Isidro, Madrid. Another of his important works is the altarpiece of *The Holy Family*, about 1655, unfolding the theme of *The Two Trinities* on the main canvas, and on the ceiling, *The Martyrdom of the Jesuits in Japan*. It is clear that the sober architectural design of the altarpiece is also by Herrera. None of his creative work was entirely original; even the best showed a clear relationship with the well-known style of Alonso Cano. His sketches are his most important works. Some are merely plans for the altars of the Chapel of S. Isidro, Madrid, and of the Church of the Virgin de Las Reyes, Toledo. Others, such as *Gabriel* and *Judith*, are splendid sketches in which a sure and delicate pen, as well as a magnificent grace and fluidity, are observed.

G. Kubler and M. Soria   Art and Architecture in Spain and Portugal   London, 1959

HIS WORKS INCLUDE

The Altarpiece of the Epiphany,
about 1450
Vich, Mus.

The St. Augustine Altarpiece,
about 1463-85
Barcelona, Mus. of Art

See also page 221

JAIME HUGUET   about 1418-1492

The last important Catalan Gothic painter to be untouched by outside influences

In 1434 Pedro Huguet came to Barcelona from Valls in Tarragona, where he was an artist as well as an agent to a painter. In Barcelona he lived near Bernardo Martorell's studio, and painted the stonework of the cathedral. Jaime Huguet, probably his son, was born in Valls. He was about 16 at the time of the move to Barcelona. At 17, he began to study painting there, learning both from his father and Martorell.

In 1440, Jaime Huguet probably went to Aragón for seven years, living in Saragossa; then he spent a year in Tarragona. All this time he was painting sad, insubstantial figures which were overpowered by the carving and gilded stucco work which surrounded them.

In 1448 he returned to Barcelona, and joined the Guild of St. Stephen. He was its president several times. He started a workshop and accepted so many orders and so many apprentices that he eventually had to have several partners. His closest associates and friends were a family called Vergos, who brought a systematized use of gilt decoration in their painting to the level of an industry.

It is said that Huguet never refused an order. Within three years of his arrival in Barcelona he was sending his altarpieces to patrons as far away as Sardinia. When he married in 1454 the ceremony took place in Barcelona Cathedral and one of his brothers, who was a priest, officiated.

In 1464 Pedro, the condestable of Portugal, landed at Barcelona, proclaimed himself king of Aragón, and surrounded himself with a brilliant court. In 1465 he asked Huguet to assist with the new decorations for the palace, and to provide an altar for the Royal Chapel. Next year the condestable died, but Huguet's altar was finished—a masterpiece of the virtues of his mature style. This style revealed strong, quiet drawing, and effectively realistic movement within the Gothic limits imposed by his conventional patrons.

The size of Huguet's studio, helped by the Vergos' productive efficiency, enabled it to outlast the economic depression which followed the restoration in 1470 of the rightful king of Aragón, Juan II. Though he had seen *The Madonna of the Councilors* in Barcelona nearly 50 years before, a work which Luis Dalmáu had painted in oils, Huguet persisted in the tempera technique that he had perfected.

B. Rowland Jr. Jaime Huguet: A Study of Late Gothic Painting in Catalonia Cambridge, Mass., 1932

Retable of the Angel and St. Bernardine of Siena (detail) 1466
Barcelona, Cath.

St. George and the Princess (detail) before 1448
Barcelona, Mus. of Art

Retable of St. Abdon and St. Sennen (detail) about 1460
Tarrasa, S. Pedro

St. Vincent Ferrer
Valencia, Cath.

HIS WORKS INCLUDE

St. Martin and the Beggar
1447 or 1457
Segorbe, Diocesan Mus.

St. Anne
Valencia, College de Játiva

St. Francis Founding his Order
Naples, S. Lorenzo

See also page 220

JAIME BAÇO, called JACOMART   1410-1461

A favorite at court for decorative paintings typical of the Valencian School

About ten years before Jaime Baço was born, his father, also called Jaime Baço, came from France to settle in Valencia. In 1400, still unused to the Spanish laws, he was brought before the authorities for disobeying a sumptuary law. By profession he was a tailor, and was employed at the court of the king of Aragón. His son, who was nicknamed Jacomart because of his Picard origin, began to be sent by the king on secret missions while he was still very young. In 1440, Jacomart was so well known and so busy with orders that he could not accept when King Alfonso V of Aragón, who was at the time besieging Naples, invited him to join the court encamped there. In 1442 there was a more urgent request, and the official title of court painter was bestowed on him. A month or two after receiving this request, he arrived in Naples, leaving behind several works still in progress. In September, 1444, Jacomart finished a painting for the king to celebrate the conquest of Naples.

The following year Jacomart made a short visit to Spain in July, 1445, when the Spanish army was at Tivoli near Rome. He painted 20 banners for the army and a large standard for the king. By 1451 Jacomart was back in Valencia, this time to stay. He was loaded with orders and honors, and painted for Valencia Cathedral and many other churches. He was made a city councilor and inspector of wine and vintages in Valencia for the year 1452-53.

Jacomart died on July 16, 1461, leaving an altarpiece unstarted which he had contracted to paint for the Cati Church. Juan Reixach, a friend, collaborator, and a pupil so imitative that his work is often difficult to distinguish from his master's, took over the entire project. Five years later he, too, was honored at court with the title of king's painter.

The style of Jacomart's art, surprisingly untouched by influences encountered on his visits to Italy, was traditional to the Valencian region. His large restrained figures are arranged on gold backgrounds among lavish brocades and glittering ornaments. The monumentally stiff figure of St. Martin in the center of the great altarpiece at Segorbe is typical of Jacomart. His landscape backgrounds, which he prettified and repeated until they became a facile trademark, are in the same purely decorative spirit. Jacomart was most concerned with the smaller, narrative compartments of an altar, like those of the St. Martin group. In these he evolved a gentleness and intimacy that overflowed into poetry.

JUAN DE JUANES   between 1520 and 1523-1579

A Valencian painter and tapestry designer well-known for his piety

Juan de Juanes was born probably at Fuente la Higuera near Valencia, the son of the painter Juan Vicente Masip. He was his father's pupil and collaborated with him from about 1535 until Masip's death in Valencia in 1550. De Juanes was originally called Vicente Juan Masip, after his father, but changed his name because of a remote relationship with the de Juanes family, whose coat of arms he used.

For his paintings de Juanes mostly chose sacred subjects, and the devotion with which he executed them became proverbial. It was said that he never missed the Sacraments before embarking on any painting for a church, and one Madonna of his at Valencia was thought to work miracles. De Juanes was also a portrait painter. Among other commissions was one for the design of tapestries to be made in Flanders for the Church of S. Tomás at Villanueva. The patron for whom he painted his masterpiece, *The Mystical Marriage*, was the Venerable Agnesio, humanist, Greek and Hebrew scholar, and a teacher and generous member of the cathedral chapter at Valencia.

In 1579 de Juanes had just finished the high altar of the Bocairente Church near Valencia, when he fell ill. He made his will, which still exists, and died on December 21st. He was buried in Bocairente, but his last wish had been to be buried in the Church of S. Cruz in Valencia, and after three years his body was carried back to his home town. His three children, Vicente Juan, Dorotea, and Margarita, all painters, were pupils of their father.

De Juanes seems to have been a timid man and traveled little. His artistic development was based almost exclusively on a continuation of his father's style. Masip had traveled once in Italy, and from that time the influence of Raphael and the great Venetians was evident in his well-defined compositions. He is, in many ways, a more interesting painter than his son.

De Juanes had his father's skill with movement and volumes. His piety tended to produce some weaknesses—blurred outlines, a melodramatic pose, or a semi-mannerist sentimentality. But at other times, as in *The Mystical Marriage*, the tenderness is less obtrusive, less sophisticated, and consequently more impressive.

G. Kubler and M. Soria   Art and Architecture in Spain and Portugal   London, 1959

The Martyrdom of St. Stephen, about 1570
Madrid, Prado

HIS WORKS INCLUDE

The Saviour
Madrid, Prado

The Last Supper
Madrid, Prado

The Assumption
Valencia, Mus. de B. A.

See also page 227

JUAN DE JUNI   about 1507-1577

A sculptor known for the Baroque quality of his work

It is supposed that Juan de Juni was born about 1507 in Joiny, a French village in the Champagne district. It is probable that he spent his apprenticeship in Italy before going to Spain. It seems as if, from the beginning, he wished to pass himself off as a Spaniard. From 1533, de Juni worked in León, in 1536 in Villalón, and in 1537 in Toro. In 1538 he started his work in Medina de Ríoseco, a city that preserves some of his most important productions.

In Zamora in 1540 he fell gravely ill. He recovered, however, and moved to Valladolid. He had a son, Isaac de Juni, who was also a sculptor, but the artist who inherited his style and clientele was Esteban Jordán.

The art of Juan de Juni, with clear Burgundian elements and noticeable Italian

St. Anne (detail)
Valladolid, Provincial Mus.

influence, always had a definite tendency toward movement and dynamic expressiveness. Paradoxically, these traits were later considered to be the hallmarks of the Valladolid School of sculpture. These characteristics and others—like clothing formed in a series of waves, diagonal postures, and the construction of groups either in enveloping curves or in broken and zig-zag silhouettes—produced a type of Baroque *avant la lettre*, that is to say, before the real age of the Baroque.

In 1539 de Juni completed *The Burial of Christ* for the Church of S. Francisco in Valladolid. It is a great sculpture in painted wood with no less than seven distorted, "Baroque" figures. The subject, definitely taken from Jacopo Florentino, was later repeated by de Juni in another work of somewhat more moderate tones for Segovia Cathedral. He died in Valladolid on April 8 or 9, 1577.

Infanta Juana of Austria, 1574
Madrid, Monastery of Descalzas Reales

POMPEO LEONI   about 1530-1608

A versatile and talented sculptor who excelled in funeral monuments

Pompeo Leoni was the son of Leone Leoni, a sculptor from Arezzo. It is presumed that he was born about 1530. In 1548 he was assisting his father, who was established in Milan near the court of Prince Philip, later Philip II. In 1557, Pompeo Leoni was appointed to the position of royal sculptor. From that time his work consisted of finishing the bronze statues made by his father in his Milan workshop. In 1558, the younger Leoni was tried by the Inquisition, and was fortunate in receiving only a light sentence for one accused of holding Lutheran beliefs. He later went to Madrid, where he married Doña Estefanía Pérez de Mora.

Leoni had a natural talent for sculpture. His training was obtained at home, and later enriched by his numerous journeys to Italy, Austria, and the Netherlands, during which he learned the varied sculptural techniques. As a result, his skill was as great with marble as with bronze. His greatest works are probably the bronze groups of Charles V and Philip II accompanied by their respective families. Their life-like pose of kneeling at prayer lends an overwhelming majesty to the vast church of the Escorial.

From the period 1576 to 1582 Leoni worked on two admirable funeral monuments: one of the inquisitor-general, Cardinal Don Diego de Espinosa, a statue in an attitude of prayer, the second of another inquisitor, Don Fernando de Valdés. In this work the ecclesiastic is accompanied by two ministers of the Inquisition. The dignity of the figures, the solemnity of their bearing, and the perfect handling of the marble are typical characteristics of Leoni's best works. His funeral sculpture started a school in Spain, and throughout the 17th century he had a large number of followers. Leoni died in Madrid on October 9, 1608, and was buried in the Church of S. Francisco el Grande.

B. G. Proske   *Pompeo Leoni*   New York, *1956*
J. Pope-Hennessy   *Italian High Renaissance and Baroque Sculpture*   London, *1958*

PEDRO MACHUCA

died 1550

A painter, architect, and sculptor who embodied all that was most Italian in the Spanish Renaissance

The Deposition (detail) after 1520
Madrid, Prado

Pedro Machuca was born in Toledo, but left for Italy before the art of his own country marked his style. There is an old tradition that he was a pupil of Raphael, but if this is true, he could not have been an industrious one. Few marks of Raphael's influence are discernible in his work. Probably he went to Parma instead and learned from the young Antonio Correggio his use of deep shadows, and his *sfumato* technique of softening and blending the edges of forms. Later Machuca did some painting in Spoleto. One large panel remains from this period, *The Madonna of Intercession*, an Italian subject painted under the influence of Italian art. He had been impressed at Orvieto by Luca Signorelli's frescoes, which included a procession of the damned into hell. He appropriated this theme, putting it into his picture as the procession of mortals into purgatory, and emphasized it with an encircling blaze of light.

Machucha did not return to Spain till after 1517. By 1520 he had settled in Granada and found the small beginnings of a large clientèle that appreciated his Italian polish. He was an excellent draftsman, and his compositions were original and fashionable. Although at first he was forced to take orders for coloring sculpture, a year later, in 1521, he collaborated on three panels that were to enshrine an altarpiece by Dieric Bouts in the Chapel of the Holy Cross in Granada. He also painted at Toledo and in the great monastery of the Military Order of Santiago at Uclés. As an architect, he made the design for the palace of Charles V which was begun in 1527 in the grounds of the Alhambra. As a sculptor and practiced appraiser, he received in 1548 an invitation in words of sugary praise to make an evaluation of Alonso Berruguete's sculpture of *The Transfiguration* in Toledo Cathedral. Two years later, on July 4, 1550, with his reputation still at its height, he died. A son, Luis Machuca, was also an architect.

C. R. Post   *A History of Spanish Painting, Vol. X   Cambridge, Mass., 1930-58*
G. Kubler and M. Soria   *Art and Architecture in Spain and Portugal   London, 1956*

HIS WORKS INCLUDE

Three Panels for an Altarpiece, 1521
Granada, Royal Chapel

The Crucifixion
Madrid, Prado

See also page 226

BERNARDO MARTORELL

died about 1453

A polished painter, illuminator, and stained-glass designer of the Catalan School

HIS WORKS INCLUDE

The St. George Altarpiece, about 1430
Chicago, Art Inst.;
Paris, Louvre

The St. Peter Altarpiece, about 1437
Pubol, Cath.

The Retable of the Transfiguration
1449-52
Barcelona, Cath.

The painter of *The St. George Altarpiece* and other works was known only as the Master of St. George until a few years ago, when a record disclosed his identity as Bernardo Martorell. First mention of Martorell is in 1433, when he was busy with a studio and had made a reputation in Barcelona. Orders for his work increased from then on, so that many pupils were necessary to help deal with them until the end of his life. His commissions included illuminations and drawings for stained glass, as

Jesus and the Samaritan (detail): from
the Retable of the Transfiguration,
1449-52
Barcelona, Cath.

well as painted altarpieces. In 1437 he had at least two important commissions for altarpieces, one of *St. Mark* and another of *St. Peter.* In 1456, three years after his death, one of his pupils arranged to take over the studio for five years and complete any paintings that were still unfinished.

Martorell painted in tempera. After the death, about 1424, of the Catalan painter Luis Borrassá, he continued to work in the International Gothic tradition which Borrassá himself had inherited from the Serra brothers. By adapting it to his own very individual artistic aims, he made himself the leading painter in Catalonia for the next 25 years. His designs do not have the vigor of Borrassá's, but the drawing is exquisitely controlled and the detail is calmly perfect—especially incidental detail such as the monkey on his rope and the dogs and ducks in *The Transfiguration,* 1449-52.

A certain dream-like quality is emphasized by Martorell's inward gazing faces. At the same time, by careful, even laborious perspectives and by differentiations of tone, he gave his compositions depth and unity, making them the climax of primitive Catalan painting.

J. Lassaigne Spanish Painting, Vol. I Geneva, 1952

The Trial of St. George (detail)
about 1430
Paris, Louvre

St. George Being Pulled to the Block
(detail) about 1430
Paris, Louvre

Decapitation of St. George (detail)
about 1430
Chicago, Art Inst.

LUIS EGIDIO MELÉNDEZ or MENÉNDEZ 1716-1780

A still-life painter at the Spanish court

Luis Meléndez was the son of Francisco Antonio Meléndez, a much traveled painter. The father worked in the first half of the 18th century to found an academy for the promotion and control of artistic activity in Spain, like those he had seen in the other great art centers of Europe. In 1726 he made a representation on the subject to the king, but died just before the Real Academia de San Fernando was finally founded in Madrid in 1751.

Luis Meléndez was born in 1716 at Naples. He was taken by his father to Madrid while quite small. With his elder sister and younger brother, who both became miniaturists, he had painting lessons from his father. Later he was sent to Rome to study the great Italian painters. When he returned to Spain he presented two pictures to King Charles III. For Fernando VI he made paintings in choir books for the Royal Chapel, and, in 1773, he painted a miniature, *The Holy Family*, for the Prince of Asturias.

Meléndez died in Madrid in 1780. A prolific painter, he had produced some effective portraits, but almost the whole of his output consisted of still-lifes of fruit, vegetables, and all the paraphernalia of the kitchen. Between 1760 and 1772 he painted 44 of these for one room of the royal palace at Aranjuez, near Madrid.

Meléndez's interest in making book paintings and miniatures is one manifes-

Self-portrait, 1745
Paris, Louvre

Still-life with Melon and Pears
Boston, Mass., Mus. of Fine Arts

Still-life: Ham, Eggs, and Bread
(detail) 1772   *Madrid, Prado*

tation of the meticulous precision that he brought to all his work. He created a naturalism so flawless, and so different from that of his French contemporary Jean Baptiste Siméon Chardin, that without the warm colors and the swelling volumes which he used, it would appear detached and cold.

Meléndez was the greatest of a line of specialists in still-life that went back to the beginning of the 17th century in Madrid. He has a special place in the history of Spanish painting, since he worked at the time of the brilliantly promising Madrid School that finished at the end of the 18th century with the early deaths of its members and the rise of Goya.

J. Lassaigne Spanish Painting, Vol. II Geneva, 1952
G. Kubler and M. Soria Art and Architecture in Spain and Portugal London, 1959

María Dolorosa, 1673
Madrid, Monastery of Descalzas Reales

PEDRO DE MENA   1628-1688

A sculptor who captured the beauty of religious pathos

Pedro de Mena was born in Granada in August, 1628, the son of the sculptor Alonso de Mena and Doña Juana de Medrano. It is likely that he learned the art of sculpture from his father. He married Doña Catalina Victoria in 1652, the year when Alonso Cano returned to Granada. At that time a close collaboration between Cano and de Mena began. This association did not prevent the latter from taking charge of a number of important commissions, but his works were saturated with Cano's style. Although *The Immaculate Conception of Alhedin* is beautiful and charming, the influence of Cano is clearly discernible.

On May 1, 1663, de Mena moved to Toledo, where he was appointed official sculptor to the cathedral. In 1664, however, he was once again in Granada, where he probably remained until 1673, when he was due to go to Cordova. Instead, de Mena went to Malaga, where he bought a house in 1674.

De Mena's largest undertaking, the choir stalls of Malaga Cathedral, consisting of no less than 40 statues, not counting another 19 by his co-workers, is far below the standard of his later excellence. Much more important are such statues as the *St. Francis of Assisi*, dignified in its exaggerated verticality, or *The Penitent Magdalen*, 1664, an excellent work that was the subject of later imitations. The sinner, with her long hair and dress of rough wool, looks despairingly at a Crucifixion. One of de Mena's most charming works is *The Madonna of Bethlehem*, an enchanting figure of maternal feeling that was obviously influenced by Cano.

Unfortunately, de Mena did not create a school, and as he worked more or less without disciples the possibility of a new generation of sculptors in Malaga passed with him. De Mena died there on October 13, 1688.

G. Kubler and M. Soria Art and Architecture in Spain and Portugal London, 1959

JUAN DE MESA

about 1586-1627

A Sevillian sculptor known for his expressive faces

Juan de Mesa was born in Cordova about 1586. He was orphaned at an early age, and went to Seville to enter the workshop of Juan Martínez Montañés in 1606. In 1607 he signed a contract of apprenticeship with Montañés for three years, and became a master sculptor by 1610. His first known statue is that of *St. Joseph and Child*, about 1615, in which he remained faithful to the style of Montañés. His greatest works, a series of Crucifixions, reflect the tradition of his teacher, in spite of their plasticity.

Most of these Crucifixions were destined for use by religious brotherhoods during Seville's Holy Week. The one of *Christ of the Good Death* is considered to be the most serene of his works. His *Crucifixion*, 1622, for the Church of St. Isabel, is unlike the others in its agonized, Baroque tension. The one in the Church of S. Pedro in Vergara is beautiful in the tragic vehemence of the imploring head, and is one of the most successful of all Spanish sculptures of the 17th century. The heads of these Crucifixions are in fact the best features of de Mesa's work, for the naked body is less carefully created and the legs are usually too thin. These qualities differentiate de Mesa's pieces from those of his great master; Montañés was always concerned with precise anatomical detail.

De Mesa's debt to Montañés was very great, and his seeming lack of originality hampered his reputation a great deal. Unfortunately, little is known of de Mesa's private life. He died in Seville in 1627.

G. Kubler and M. Soria   Art and Architecture in Spain and Portugal   London, 1959

Christ Recumbent
Seville, S. Gregorio

HIS WORKS INCLUDE

Christ of the Good Death, about 1619
Seville, University Chapel
Jesús del Gran Poder, 1620
Seville, S. Lorenzo
The Crucifixion, 1622
Seville, S. Isabel

See also page 283

JUAN MARTÍNEZ MONTAÑÉS

1568-1649

Spain's greatest wood carver

Juan Martínez Montañés was born in Alcalá la Real, Jaén province, where he was baptized on March 16, 1568. He moved to Granada about 1580 to become an apprentice to Pablo de Rojas. It seems that Montañés arrived in Seville in 1582, and in 1587 he married Doña Ana de Villegas. In 1588 Montañés passed the examinations for master sculptor, and from then on dedicated himself entirely to his profession. In 1591 he became involved in an unpleasant affair concerning the death of one of his employees. It is not clear whether it was murder or an accident, but he went to prison. Montañés was released in 1593 after a pardon from the dead man's widow. In 1612 his wife died, and eight months later he married Doña Catalina de Sandoval. In 1629 Montañés fell gravely ill and was confined to bed for five months; however, he slowly recuperated from his illness. In June, 1635, he

Sepulcher of Don Alfonso Pérez de Guzmán (detail) 1610-13
Santiponce, Spain, Monastery of
S. Isidro del Campo

195

traveled to Madrid to model a portrait of Philip IV, almost the only big journey of his life. Montañés died in his adopted city of Seville of the plague, and was buried there on June 18, 1649.

Montañés' long life was used fully, and he produced a vast quantity of work. His statues were usually executed in wood, and afterwards gilded and oil painted. It is noteworthy that much of Montañés' work was painted by his friend Francisco Pacheco. Apart from the statues of Don Alonso Pérez de Guzmán and Doña María Coronel in prayer at the Monastery of S. Isidro del Campo in Santiponce, all his known subjects are religious. Before he started these works, Montañés had already gained his reputation with a true *capolavoro* (masterpiece), *Christ on the Cross*, commissioned in 1603 by Archdeacon Vázquez de Leca for Seville Charterhouse, and now in the cathedral. After its completion it was justly considered the most perfect Spanish example of this great subject.

G. Kubler and M. Soria   Art and Architecture in Spain and Portugal   London, 1959

Christ on the Cross (detail)
Granada, S. José

JOSÉ DE MORA   1642-1724

A sculptor who brought the Granada School to the fore

José de Mora was born in Baza, Granada province, on February 26, 1642, the son of Bernardo de Mora and Damiana López Criado. When he was ten years old, de Mora moved to Granada with his family. There he executed his first works in the style of Alonso Cano, the great artist of the city. About 1667 he left for Madrid, and worked there in a style similar to that of Sebastián de Herrera Barnuevo. In 1673 de Mora was in Granada once more. He married his cousin Doña Louisa de Mena y Herrera on September 24, 1685. De Mora enjoyed great esteem as a sculptor. On January 25, 1704, Doña Louisa died, and the loss must have unbalanced him. He survived her by 20 years, submerged in a gentle and peaceful insanity that lasted until his death in Granada on October 25, 1724.

De Mora's subject matter is exclusively religious and does not differ significantly from that of the other Granada sculptors, such as Pedro de Mena and Cano. It includes various versions of the Immaculate Conception, Ecce Homo, the Virgin of Sorrows, the Virgin of Solitude, and the Crucifixion. Nevertheless, de Mora departed considerably from the usual tone found in Andalusian images, for his work is quieter and less spectacular than that of his teachers and contemporaries. He preferred dramatic themes, but always handled them with the greatest restraint, trying to overcome suffering with charm and flexibility.

One of de Mora's major works is *The Immaculate Conception* in the Church of S. Justo y Pastor in Granada, a sad version in the the tradition of Cano. The most famous of his creations is *Christ on the Cross*. It is clean-limbed, beautiful in line, noble, and almost Hellenic in conception.

G. Kubler and M. Soria   Art and Architecture in Spain and Portugal   London, 1959

LUIS DE MORALES between 1520 and 1525-1586

A purely Mannerist painter

Luis de Morales was born and lived all his life in the city of Badajoz in the province of Estremadura. There, men grew up to be soldiers, small farmers, or adventurers, but not, before Morales, artists. So it was natural that he should evolve a primarily emotional style, quite separate from the mainstream of Spanish art.

There were at that time many Spanish teachers in Valladolid and Toledo to whom he could have gone, but he evidently found his early inspiration in Flemish pictures, like those of Quentin Massys. These were admired for their realism, and were collected in Portugal, just over the border from Estremadura.

Morales' own virtues, which after his death gave rise to the popular nickname of "El Divino," were a profound faith and an all-pervasive piety. Even these failed him when he restricted himself to a handful of traditional subjects, which he repeated over and over again in the hope of intensifying their significance each time. His output was huge. The expressions, gestures, and details in his pictures began to be overdone, and the thin figures, lengthened faces, and merging edges of his Mannerist style only conveyed a facile melancholy sentiment.

Morales went only once to Madrid—when he was asked by Philip II to provide a sample of his work with a view to a commission of paintings for the Escorial. He offered a *Carrying of the Cross*. But as Philip had been brought up to appreciate the great Venetians and preferred a more classical style, the picture failed to please him. It was accepted instead for the Church of St. Jerome in Madrid. Morales returned home disillusioned, to paint sad subjects in thin colors. He married, and his first son was born when he was 45 years old. In the same year he was paid for an altarpiece for Badajoz Cathedral.

Morales' pictures were immensely popular with ordinary people if not with the court. Toward the end of his long life he was inexplicably poor. But for the last five years he had a pension of 300 ducats, granted him by King Philip when they met again in 1581, this time in Badajoz.

For more than a generation after his death in 1586, many pictures imitating Morales' themes and mannerisms were made. His reputation has therefore suffered.

E. du G. Trapier Luis de Morales and Leonardesque Influence in Spain New York, 1933
G. Kubler and M. Soria Art and Architecture in Spain and Portugal London, 1959

The Blessed Juan de Ribera
Madrid, Prado

HIS WORKS INCLUDE

The Madonna and Child with a Bird, 1546
Madrid, S. Augustin

The Madonna and Child
Madrid, Prado

St. Stephen
Madrid, Prado

The Visitation
Badojoz, Cath.

See also page 228

BARTOLOMÉ ESTEBAN MURILLO 1617-1682

A painter variously called the Raphael and the van Dyck of Spanish art

At the end of 1617 in Seville, where Diego Velázquez and Francisco de Zurbarán had just finished their apprenticeships, Bartolomé Esteban Murillo was born into a family in which the name Esteban Murillo was common. His father, Gaspar

Self-portrait (detail) about 1678
London, N. G.

Dolorosa, about 1655-70
Madrid, Prado

A Peasant Boy Leaning on a Sill,
late work   *London, N. G.*

Esteban Murillo, and his mother, María Pérez, had him baptized on New Year's Day, 1618. When he was ten years old they died, leaving him in the care of an uncle in whose house he first indulged and expanded his talent for painting. He produced devotional pictures in watercolor or tempera on thin canvas that were always possible to sell for the Seville fairs, or for export to the Spanish colonies in South America. This small trade continued when his uncle apprenticed him to the painter Juan del Castillo, another relative and also the teacher of Alonso Cano. Murillo learned the principle as well as the practice of drawing and painting. When Castillo moved to Cadiz, Murillo was left free to carry out all the orders for popular subjects that the picture dealers sent him.

On February 26, 1645, in the Seville Church of S. María Magdalena in which he had been baptized, Murillo married Doña Beatriz de Cabrera, a woman of substance with some land in the town of Pilas, where she was born. A domesticized Murillo did his first serious and successful work in 1645-46 — 11 paintings for the little cloister of the Seville Convent of St. Francis.

Murillo longed to travel, but he was too proud to borrow his wife's money for this purpose. Instead he bought a large canvas, and cut it into small pieces. These he used for a series of miniature holy pictures, which he sold to a shipper to the West Indies. Mass production at this stage risked spoiling the rich style that he was beginning to achieve. It is doubtful if Murillo ever got as far as Madrid because he found it so difficult to be away from his work.

Murillo was able to establish his Sevillian workshop as a significant factor in the art world of his day. Orders poured in, and he took on many assistants, whom he taught with the gentleness natural both to his character and his work. The realism of his own Madonnas, urchins, peddlers, portraits, and saints — his Madonnas are young Andalusian girls, and *St. Isidore and St. Leander* of 1655, in Seville Cathedral, are the larger than life size portraits of two scholars — is tempered with an air of charm, grace, and tenderness.

Under the sheer momentum of Murillo's virtuosity, the realism sometimes degenerated into a merely facile sentiment, but it is, nevertheless, the unifying element in his huge output. From Ribera's pictures he had learned to give his subjects body by means of a masterly placing of light and shadow, but his forms have none of the starkness of Zurbarán's. Murillo's light is warm, his shadows cool. His coloring, inspired by the Flemish and Venetian colorists, is delicate and subtle.

The ultimate test of Murillo's temperate nature was the projected institution of a public academy of drawing in Seville. In a patient campaign to persuade the artists of the city to help him bear the expense of such a school he had to contend with the professional jealousy and bad temper of Juan de Valdés Leal and the younger Francisco Herrera. Finally he was able to arrange the first session in the municipal buildings on January 11, 1660. He and Herrera were joint directors and Valdés Leal was made treasurer. Murillo gave public lessons there in drawing the human anatomy from a nude model, thus creating a precedent in Seville.

In 1662 Murillo applied for membership of the lay brotherhood of La Caridad, a Seville society that had been founded about 150 years earlier to help the poor and bury the dead. He was admitted, after a long inquiry, in 1665, and later commissioned, with Valdés Leal, to decorate its newly reconstructed church. His reputation and popularity were in fact enormous, but they never affected his simple, vocational attitude to his art and life. When an *Immaculate Conception* of his was shown in Madrid on the feast day of Corpus Christi, 1670, he was invited to court by the king, but he refused, pleading his age as an excuse.

12 years later, when he was at Cadiz painting the huge *Mystical Marriage of St. Catherine* for the altar of the Capuchin Convent there, Murillo slipped and fell from his scaffolding, injuring himself. He had to return to Seville, where he lingered on for a month or two, sick and apparently a little crazy. He often went to the nearby Church of S. Cruz and prayed before a picture of *The Descent from the Cross*. When the sacristan asked him why he spent so much time there he said that he was waiting for the holy gentlemen to finish taking Christ down from the cross. On April 3, 1682, he died and was buried in the chapel where this picture hung. His great fortune was left to his two sons, Gabriel, who was a priest in America, and Gaspar, a painter and canon in Seville.

Though Murillo himself had never left Spain, such a steady foreign market for his pictures existed that Charles IV forbade Spanish customs officials to let them out of the country, but even this failed to stop the stream. In the Seville School his influence was dominant, if in a disfigured form, for a century and a half.

C. B. Curtis Velázquez and Murillo London and New York, 1883

HIS WORKS INCLUDE

The Angels' Kitchen, 1646
Paris, Louvre

The Last Supper, 1650
Seville, S. María la Blanca

St. Isidore and St. Leander, 1655
Seville, Cath.

Appearance of Christ to St. Augustine, about 1655
Minneapolis, Minn., Walker Art Center

The Vision of St. Anthony, 1656
Seville, Cath.

Series, 1665-70
Seville, Capuchin Convent

Santiago Madonna, about 1675
New York, Met. Mus.

The Mystical Marriage of St. Catherine, 1682
Cadiz, Capuchin Convent

The Two Trinities, about 1682
London, N. G.

See also pages 246, 247

BARTOLOMÉ ORDÓÑEZ   about 1480-1520

An exquisite sculptor of the Spanish Renaissance

Bartolomé Ordóñez was born into a noble family in Burgos about 1480. After a preliminary education in his own district, he became a disciple of Domenico Alejandro Fancelli, and took over a number of tasks that had been entrusted to this sculptor from Settignano, including the tombs of Philip I and Juana for the Royal Chapel in Granada. It is possible that Ordóñez was also a disciple, or follower at least, of Andrea Sansovino. At all events, it seems that he spent some time studying in Rome and also visited Naples. This was before 1515, when he was definitely established in Barcelona as the head of a workshop, where the collaborators and assistants were all Italians.

On May 7, 1517, Ordóñez signed a contract with the ruling body of Barcelona Cathedral for an important commission. He was to decorate the end panels of the choir stalls and to build a great marble *trascoro* (a wall at the west end of the choir). The carvings of the end panels of the high and low stalls at the front, and those on the high stalls facing the high altar, were soon completed with the aid of the

The Sale of Joseph: from the Choir Stalls, 1517-19 *Barcelona, Cath.*

199

Frenchman Jean Monet. Ordóñez was probably helped by Diego de Siloe as well, and the work on the stalls was finished about the end of 1517. This was the date when he contracted to buy 93 cartloads of marble from a stonecutter of Carrara. Indubitably, some of this material was destined for the task on which he was working throughout the whole of 1518—the altarpiece of the Caracciolo di Vico Chapel in the Church of S. Giovanni di Carbonara. This altarpiece, featuring a beautiful central bas-relief of *The Epiphany*, is carved with an unbelievable delicacy.

The greater part of the marble bought in Carrara was intended for the *trascoro* of Barcelona Cathedral, to which city Ordóñez returned at the beginning of 1519. There he married Catalina Calaf on February 22 of the same year. Although the artist was not able to finish his work on the *trascoro*, he did complete two reliefs of great beauty, *St. Eulalia before the Roman Prefect* and *The Martyrdom of St. Eulalia*. Ordóñez died in the prime of life in December, 1520.

H. E. Wethey   The Early Works of Bartolomé Ordóñez and Diego de Siloe   New York, 1943
B. G. Proske   Castilian Sculpture, Gothic to Renaissance   New York, 1951

The Martyrdom of St. Denis, 1484
Valencia, Cath.

RODRIGO DE OSONA   died after 1510

A busy and successful painter in Valencia in the last quarter of the 14th century

As a very young man Rodrigo de Osona was probably in northern Italy, studying in Padua and, with his contemporary Ercole de' Roberti, in Bologna or Ferrara. In 1475 he went to Flanders, and learned a great deal from the work of Hugo van der Goes, then established as dean of the guild in Ghent. He also benefited from pictures by other Flemish artists, including Roger van der Weyden and Dieric Bouts.

By 1476, de Osona was an established painter in Valencia, and on April 20th of that year, Juan Albarraci, the vicar of the Church of St. Nicholas, commissioned him for an altarpiece. The style of *The Crucifixion* that he painted is already fully developed, showing some influence from his experience of Flemish art. For example, the medium is oil, and episodes secondary to the main theme are incorporated into the pictures. The sure drawing technique must have been perfected in Flanders. Other features, such as the two-tone painting of the predella panel, that gives the effect of classical sculptured reliefs, are Italian. The influence of Hugo van der Goes can be seen in the vigorous individualization of the male figures, and that of Ercole de' Roberti in the still beauty of the women. All the sadness in de Osona's paintings and the undertones of meaning are his own and very Spanish. So is the realism of the landscape backgrounds, and the sophisticated narrowness of his figures. The almost too elegant forms of *The Madonna with the Montesa Knight* were the culmination of his technique.

De Osona's art was thus the natural product of his cosmopolitan training. He received many orders, but only a few of his works survive. By 1482, six years after the contract for *The Crucifixion*, he was in partnership with one of the most popular painters of the time, Pedro Cabanes. Less than two years later, from 1483 to 1484, de Osona was painting an altar in Valencia Cathedral for Cardinal Rodrigo Borgia, the future Pope Alexander VI.

A son, also named Rodrigo de Osona, was active as a painter from about 1505 to 1513, but his imitations of the father's style were never inspired. The posthumous fame of the elder Rodrigo was maintained by his studio, which for 50 years was the most productive in Valencia.

J. Lassaigne   Spanish Painting, Vol. I   Geneva, 1952

FRANCISCO PACHECO   1564-1644

An intellectual artist who was the teacher of Diego Velázquez

Francisco Pacheco, son of Juan Pérez and Leonor de los Ríos, was born in Sanlúcar, Seville province, in 1564. While still a youth he went to Seville, where he was an apprentice in the workshop of the painter Luis Fernández. From 1594, commissions rained upon Pacheco both from the city of Seville and the outlying districts, thanks to the wide social circles in which he moved. In 1598, along with other colleagues, he worked on the monument erected by the cathedral for the funeral of Philip II. In the same year Pacheco married María del Páramo.

Joachim and Anna at the Golden Gate
Budapest, Mus. of Fine Arts

In 1611 he visited Madrid, the Escorial, and Toledo, and from 1618, as censor of religious paintings, he was always concerned, almost obsessed, that they should be realistic. Pacheco is an example of the intellectual artist, that is to say he was the friend of aristocrats, artists, musicians, and poets. For a long time it was thought that he had lived until 1654, but a recent investigation of records has revealed that he died on November 27, 1644, in Seville. Pacheco's greatest claim to fame derives from his having been the teacher, and later the father-in-law, of Diego Velázquez.

Pacheco's production, rich in subject matter, reflects his academic tastes. These can be seen in his book, "The Art of Painting, Its Antiquity and Greatness," which was written slowly, appearing posthumously in 1649. This volume of art theory and criticism is more valuable than his paintings. It may be that Pacheco's lack of the gift for color is responsible for the unattractiveness of his works. Nevertheless, his sketches are extraordinarily good, which is as it should be for an academician of the 1600's. Pachecho's greatest success is his "Book Describing the True Portraits of Famous and Noteworthy Gentlemen," which contains depictions of 170 of his contemporaries with whom he maintained more or less friendly relations. They include superb sketches in red and black pencil of such geniuses as Lope de Vega, Francisco de Quevedo, Luis de Vargas, Rodrigo Caro, and Gutierre de Cetina.

G. Kubler and M. Soria   Art and Architecture in Spain and Portugal   London, 1959

HIS WORKS INCLUDE

St. Albert on his Bier, 1617
Seville, coll. Count Ibarra
Knight of Santiago, 1626
Williamstown, Mass., Lawrence Art Mus.

See also page 261

LUIS PARET Y ALCAZÁR 1746-1799

Apart from Goya, the most brilliant 18th-century painter in Spain

Luis Paret y Alcazár, son of the Frenchman, Paul Paret, and his Spanish wife, María del Pilar Alcazár, was born in Madrid on February 15, 1746. He was evidently a precocious painter as he became the pupil of the monk, Bartolomé de San Antonio, and of the jeweler, Duflos, before he was ten years old. From 1756 he studied at the Real Academia de San Fernando, where his teacher was Antonio González Velázquez. It was in this institution that, in 1760, he won a first prize. He then left for Rome, backed financially by the Infante Don Luis de Bourbon. Back again in Madrid in 1766, Paret won the first prize in the triennial competition of the academy. It was then that he painted his charming picture, *The Masked Ball.* In 1770-71 he stayed in Aranjuez and painted his great work, *The Royal Tattoo.*

In 1775, as a consequence of an unsavory incident that took place in the house of his patron, the Infante Don Luis, Paret was sentenced to exile on Puerto Rico, where he arrived probably in December of that year. On January 24, 1776, in order to beg a pardon from the king, he painted a self-portrait dressed in the clothes of an island peasant. He received his pardon in August, 1778, and arrived in Spain in the autumn of that year. In 1779 or 1780 Paret married Micaela Fourdinier. Soon after, he was elected a member of the Real Academia de San Fernando. From 1783 to 1786 he worked on numerous and varied tasks for both the municipality and private individuals in Bilbao, and in 1787-88 on similar ones in Navarre.

In 1789 Paret painted decorations of Madrid in homage to the new king, Charles IV. From 1792 he was vice-secretary to the academy, but in 1795 he suffered the disappointment of not being elected deputy director of painting in the position vacated by Francisco Bayeu. This failure embittered his last years, and Paret died on February 14, 1799.

Paret was one of the most polished Spanish painters of his day. He possessed, above all, a most delicate range of colors. His pictures, most of which are small in size, are usually peopled by a multitude of animated and charming figures, as in *The Arsenal Quay at Bilbao,* 1780.

Portrait of a Seated Lady
Barcelona, Mus. of Art

HIS WORKS INCLUDE

The Draper's Shop, 1773
Madrid, Mus. Lazáro

Charles III of Spain Dining with his Court, 1768-72
Madrid, Prado

The Prudence of Diogenes, 1780
Madrid, Real Acad. de San Fernando

The Arsenal Quay at Bilbao, 1780
Oxfordshire, England, Upton House, National Trust

The Finding of the Holy Cross
Bilbao, Mus. de B. A. y de Arte Moderno, coll. Gortazar

See also page 271

FRANCISCO RIBALTA 1565-1628

A precursor of Spanish 17th-century realism

Francisco Ribalta was born at Solsona, Lérida province. At an early age he moved with his parents to Barcelona, and worked there as a young painter. In 1582, he was painting in Madrid, and also studying Italian works at the Escorial. Although he was given no official position at the court there, he made friends with the Escorial school painter Juan Fernández de Navarrete the Deaf, and with the poet Lope de Vega. In 1614 Lope de Vega asked Ribalta to paint his portrait, and wrote verses in praise of the painter.

In 1599 the family moved to Valencia, where Ribalta did his best work. It was

HIS WORKS INCLUDE

Cycle of Paintings, 1601-10
Valencia, College of Corpus Christi

The Vision of Father Simon, 1612
London, N. G.

St. Francis Embracing Christ, about 1620
Valencia, Mus. de B. A.

St. Bernard Embracing Christ, about 1625
Madrid, Prado

See also page 262

probably a contract with Juan de Ribera, the archbishop, for the newly-founded College of Corpus Christi that took Ribalta to Valencia. He worked for this college until his death. For its high altar he painted his masterpiece, *The Last Supper*, in which the head of St. Andrew was said to be that of the Venerable Pedro Muñoz, while Judas was supposed to be a portrait of a shoemaker, Pradas, with whom Ribalta had quarreled.

From 1607 to 1617 Ribalta threw his energies into establishing a school of painters at Valencia. His own pupils, who for a time included José de Ribera, made a lasting and effective nucleus of influence there. He died in Valencia, and was buried in the Church of S. Juan del Mercado on January 14, 1628. Ribalta's son, Juan, was a painter in the style of his father (but more under the influence of the Caravaggists) and so accomplished that his works were in demand from the time he was 18. Juan died in the same year as his father, and was buried in the same church.

Francisco Ribalta's style was shaped throughout by artistic developments of his own time. These included the Mannerist influence of the pictures by Sebastiano del Piombo which he frequently copied in the Escorial. At the same time he came under the potent influence of the court painter Navarrete, and Ribalta developed a controlled but vital realism from his style. He was able to do this because of his new realization of the subtleties of human anatomy. His realistic effects were enhanced by luminism or tenebrism (the technique of making effects by brilliant light and deep shadow) which he had also learned from Navarrete. This tendency in his work was reinforced much later when, after 1615, he was well established at Valencia, and paintings by the followers of his famous Italian contemporary, Caravaggio, began to trickle into Spain.

D. F. Darby   Francisco Ribalta and his School   New York, 1952

St. Luke Painting the Virgin
(self-portrait) (detail)
Valencia, Provincial Mus.

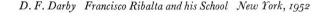

JOSÉ DE RIBERA

1591-1652

A realist painter of a concentrated, forceful observation

José de Ribera was born at Játiva, a little town in the hills south of Valencia. Before he was seven his mother died and his father remarried. Ribera was sent to Valencia to learn Latin and become a scholar, but instead he became an apprentice painter to Francisco Ribalta. Ribalta taught him his exacting naturalist technique.

When Ribera was still a boy he left Spain and went to Italy, never to return. He went straight to Rome and arrived there penniless, living on pieces of bread given to him by other students. *Il Spagnoletto* (the little Spaniard) went purposefully through the streets making studies of everything he could see. There is a story that a cardinal saw him copying a fresco on a palace façade, took pity on him and invited him back to his house. He pleased the cardinal's household and was

Boy with a Club-Foot, 1652
Paris, Louvre

asked to stay on. However, Ribera found that a new and comfortable laziness was damaging his progress, and soon returned to the streets.

For some years Ribera made a devoted study of two quite opposite styles, the classical elements of the Carracci brothers and the *chiaroscuro* of Caravaggio. He also admired the works of Raphael and Michelangelo. Then, on a trip to Parma, he made so many copies of Correggio's paintings that their influence temporarily sweetened his style. However, it was Caravaggio who permanently affected Ribera's art.

When Ribera was about 25, he went to Naples, where Caravaggio's influence proved most durable. A wealthy Neapolitan painter and picture dealer recognized his brilliant talent, and offered Ribera his daughter in marriage, with the promise of his entire fortune. When Ribera accepted, the proud father-in-law spread the news of his abilities until Ribera had a steady flow of orders and was able to support a studio of assistants.

For nearly two hundred years Naples had been under Spanish control, and at this time the viceroys sent from Spain were almost always distinguished art collectors. When the duke of Oluna, viceroy from 1616 to 1620, saw a *St. Bartholomew* by Ribera that his father-in-law had insisted on showing from the balcony of their house to a crowd gathered below, he took the artist on as his salaried court painter and gave him numerous commissions. The duke's successors did the same, and eventually Ribera was granted an apartment in the palace, where he was able to restrict his work to six hours each day, and keep open house to distinguished friends the rest of the time.

Ribera's fame reached the art circles of Rome, where he was elected in 1626 to

Jacob's Dream, 1639
Madrid, Prado

The Blind Sculptor of Gambazo, 1632
Madrid, Prado

the Academy of St. Luke and in 1648 admitted by the pope to the Military Order of Christ. When Velázquez, court painter to Philip IV of Spain, came to visit Ribera in 1630, and again 19 years later in 1649, he took away with him pictures for the royal collections.

Ribera's work thus became the main channel into Spain of the Caravaggesque. Not only did he make consistent use of Caravaggio's method of *chiaroscuro* to build up the appearance of bulk with deep shades, but he also brought Caravaggio's realism into his paintings, pen and pencil drawings, and etchings.

Ribera's martyrs, ancient gods, apostles, ecstatics, hermits, and Madonnas are human, even peasant types, vigorous and unsentimentalized, and there are many direct portrayals of beggars and cripples, as well as people with goiters and other deformities. Fortunately his patrons shared his taste for abnormalities, and the peculiarly Spanish sense of basic human dignity that went with it. It was a Spanish viceroy in Naples, the Duke of Alcalá, who suggested Ribera's portrait of the bearded woman *Magdalena Ventura*, 1631.

This aspect of Ribera's realism, always drawn from life, was the product of a fascination with the actual varying shape and texture of things, which had been cultivated in him by his first master Ribalta. It is apparent in the etched sheets of studies of eyes, ears, and mouths which he used for the instruction of his pupil-assistants.

Don Juan, the 19-year-old bastard son of Philip IV who came with the Spanish Armada to restore order in Naples, had his portrait painted by Ribera, frequented his studio, and had an affair with one of his daughters. Don Juan's callous conduct seems to have distressed Ribera, causing in about 1650 an aggravation of the ill health which had been troubling him for ten years. Two years later, on September 5, 1652, he died.

E. du G. Trapier *Ribera* New York, *1952*
J. Lassaigne *Spanish Painting, Vol. II* Geneva, *1952*

The Holy Family with St. Catherine
1648 *New York, Met. Mus.*
Samuel D. Lee Fund

Jusepe de Ribera

EDUARDO ROSALES   1836-1873

An independent working within the academic system of the 19th century

Eduardo Rosales was born in Madrid. He lived there as a boy in a state of oppressive poverty which made him a consumptive and probably caused his early death at 37. At the age of 15 he was accepted at the Real Academia de San Fernando in Madrid to make his first serious study of painting under its teachers Luis Ferrant and Federico de Madrazo.

Throughout his career Rosales was recognized by one official body after another. When he was 21 he went to Italy. In Siena and Rome he made a meticulous study of the old masters, and returned to Spain only two years before his death. He tried his hand at those historical subjects, fraught with emotion and public significance, which had come to supplant all other themes in the imagination of 19th-century painters. His canvases were huge: *The Last Testament of Isabella the Catholic* is 9 feet

HIS WORKS INCLUDE
The Countess of Santovenia
Bilbao, coll. Felix Valdés
The Duke of Fernán Nuñez
Madrid, coll. the Duke of Fernán Nuñez

See also page 256

The Last Testament of Isabella the Catholic (detail)
Madrid, Mus. de Arte Moderno

high and 13 feet long. Whereas a facile emptiness of feeling tended to be exposed by the immense proportions of his contemporaries' canvases, Rosales' original forcefulness gave his realism conviction, and his compositions an intense, effective simplicity. Size became just one more element in an imposing whole.

During Rosales' lifetime Spanish art had reached a low water mark, and by contrast his skillful handling of any material was obvious to his contemporaries. He first showed his work to appreciative viewers at the Spanish National Exhibition in Madrid, 1864, and the Paris International Exhibition, 1865. He won many awards and other honors. *The Death of Lucretia*, 1871, was bought by the state for over 5,000 dollars. In 1873, the year of his death in Madrid, he was made director of the Spanish Academy in Rome.

Rosales set ideals for himself that were diametrically opposed to the classical and romantic influences that might have suited his creative inspiration. An indication of what he might have achieved is revealed in the preliminary sketches for his paintings, and in the broad luminous style of some landscapes which he made in Murcia during the years before his death.

J. Lassaigne   Spanish Painting, Vol. II   Geneva, 1952

The Angel
Palma de Mallorca,
Business Exchange

HIS WORKS INCLUDE

St. Paul
Palma de Mallorca, Cath.

The Madonna
Palma de Mallorca,
Business Exchange

See also page 275

GUILLERMO SAGRERA   about 1375-1454

A Mallorcan sculptor who created dramatic images

The exact date of Guillermo Sagrera's birth is not known, but it is thought that he was born about 1375 in Mallorca. In 1410 he was chief craftsman responsible for the art works of Perpignan Cathedral. From 1420 he was chief craftsman in charge of the art works in Palma de Mallorca Cathedral, a position he kept until 1447. In 1422 Sagrera received a large sum of money for the statue of *St. Peter* in this cathedral.

In 1426 Sagrera signed a contract for the construction of the *Lonja* (Business Exchange) at Palma de Mallorca, a duty that, with interruptions, occupied him until 1451. He delegated much of the final work to disciples, including his cousin, Miguel Sagrera, and Guillermo Vilasolar. Nevertheless, it is known that *The Angel* and *The Madonna* of this beautiful building are the work of Sagrera. He was summoned to Naples in 1447 by Alfonso V, "the Magnanimous," who entrusted him with the construction of the New Castle the following year. He died in 1454 without finishing it, but not before he had left the mark of his very personal style on many of the ornamental details.

There are very few sculptors who have won such a great and well-merited reputation for such a small quantity of work. The Late Gothic statue of *St. Peter* in Mallorca Cathedral would justify this fame, even by itself, being a monumental and dramatic work, executed with effective grandeur. There has been mention of the relationship between Sagrera's sculpture and that of Claus Sluter, but this must be no more than a coincidental reflection of the time in which they both worked.

FRANCISCO SALZILLO

1707-1783

Murcia's gift to Spanish sculpture

Francisco Salzillo Alcaraz was born on May 21, 1707, in Murcia, son of the sculptor Nicolas Salzillo and Doña Isabel Alcaraz. His first studies were at the Jesuit College of S. Esteban, which aroused in him sufficient religious zeal to enter the Convent of S. Domingo as a novice, where he remained for seven years. On his father's death in 1727, he left to support his mother by making wood carvings and sculpture. It is known that in 1743 Salzillo married Doña Juana Vallejo y Martínez. On July 22, 1775, he was appointed municipal sculptor of Murcia.

Salzillo never left Spain, and probably not even Murcia. His work was thus exclusively destined for the clientele of this city and its district. He was assisted by his seven brothers in the workshop, which accounted for the great quantity of work produced from 1727 to 1746. These statues are lacking in variety, although a *Pietà*, 1740, stands out as an original and beautiful piece. The sculpture that Salzillo created in the years considered to be his greatest, from 1747 to 1756, was somewhat superior to his earlier works. *The Prayer in the Garden*, 1754, shows the height of the artist's inspiration. The incredible beauty of the angel surpassed any other Andalusian or Castilian creation of the time. Salzillo fell ill on February 20, 1783, died on March 2, and was buried in the Capuchin Convent.

The Fall on the Road to Calvary
1752   *Murcia, Mus. Salzillo*

HIS WORKS INCLUDE
The Prayer in the Garden, 1754
Murcia, Mus. Salzillo

See also page 287

GIL DE SILOE

died about 1505

A sculptor who worked in marble and alabaster with great delicacy

All kinds of mysteries surround the origins, dates, and life of the sculptor Gil de Siloe, who was not only one of the greatest artists of the late Middle Ages in Spain, but was also the father of Diego de Siloe. The latter started a notable epoch, in the Renaissance era, in the history of Spanish art.

It is quite certain that de Siloe's style was completely formed when in 1475 he suddenly appeared in Burgos, then a city of considerable wealth. It is supposed that about this time the sculptor started on the tomb of Bishop Don Alonso de Cartagena in the cathedral, an important work, but not as expressive of his style as his later ones. In 1486 he worked on the tomb of John II and Isabel of Portugal, and from 1489 to 1493 on the tomb of the Infante Don Alfonso, both commissions being executed in the Carthusian Monastery of Miraflores, near Burgos. From 1500 to 1503 he was employed on the tomb of the page Don Juan de Padilla for the Monastery of Fres del Val. The exact date of his death is unknown, but it was probably in Burgos about 1505.

De Siloe possessed an astonishing technique. He delighted in faithfully representing the jewelry, embroidery, and other adornments on the clothing of the people whom he immortalized. His minute detail contrasts with the smoothness and tautness of the faces and the elegance of the hands.

HIS WORKS INCLUDE
Don Antonio Manrique
Burgos, Mus.
Retable
Burgos, Carthusian Monastery

See also page 276

Transparente (detail) 1721-32
Toledo, Cath.

HIS WORKS INCLUDE

David Offered Bread and Wine
by Abimelech: relief from the
Transparente, 1721-32
Toledo, Cath.

See also page 286

NARCISO TOMÉ   about 1690-1742

A Spanish sculptor known for his Baroque altarpieces

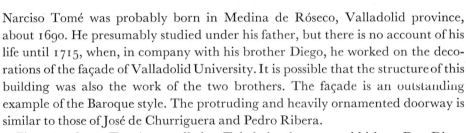

Narciso Tomé was probably born in Medina de Róseco, Valladolid province, about 1690. He presumably studied under his father, but there is no account of his life until 1715, when, in company with his brother Diego, he worked on the decorations of the façade of Valladolid University. It is possible that the structure of this building was also the work of the two brothers. The façade is an outstanding example of the Baroque style. The protruding and heavily ornamented doorway is similar to those of José de Churriguera and Pedro Ribera.

Five years later, Tomé was called to Toledo by the new archbishop, Don Diego de Astorga y Céspedes, and was entrusted with the work of the famous *Transparente*, an enormous altarpiece in the center of the apse-aisle of the Gothic cathedral. The work was illuminated by an aperture in the roof, and placed so that the light would fall upon it in a spectacular way, giving the altarpiece its name. The *Transparente* is an ornate mass of confused lines running into one another, formed by clouds, columns, rays, and bas- and high-reliefs. A skillfully mounted image of *The Madonna and Child* in the central vaulted niche shows that Tomé could also design austerely. The marble, jasper, and bronze combine to produce a dazzling effect. His last important work was the great Baroque altarpiece of Léon Cathedral, started in 1738 and finished after Tomé's death in 1742 by his relative Simón Tomé Gavitán.

The King, about 1260
Burgos, Cath.

See also page 273

THE UNKNOWN SCULPTOR OF *THE QUEEN*   about 1260

A masterpiece of the Spanish Gothic style

One of the most famous sculptures of Burgos Cathedral, and one of the masterpieces of the Spanish Gothic style, is a 13th-century figure known as *The Queen*. She stands against the wall of the high cloister, looking at her husband, *The King*, who is offering her a ring. Both are figures of striking beauty, extremely important for a study of the clothes and hair styles of about 1260. Opinions have changed about the identity of the lady. Previously she was believed to represent Beatrice of Swabia, wife of Ferdinand III. Since he died in 1252, however, it is thought that the couple might portray the royal successors, Alfonso X and Doña Violante of Aragon.

This theory would be in keeping with the style of the sculpture. It is thought that the sculptor might have been the so-called Master of the Crown, who created the statues at the north wall of the cathedral, and who, perhaps, can be identified as Master Enrique, director-in-chief of the art works in León Cathedral. This artist died in 1277, some years after the sculptures in the cloister at Burgos were executed.

JUAN DE VALDÉS LEAL

The last inspired master of the Seville School

The Triumph of Death, 1672
Seville, Hospital de La Caridad

Juan de Valdés Leal was born in 1622 in the Andalusian city of Seville. His father was a Portuguese goldsmith. His mother came from an Andalusian family called Valdés, and it was with this name that their son eventually signed his pictures— Juan Valdés. His parents took him as a little boy to Cordova, and when they discovered that he wanted to paint they sent him to master Antonio del Castillo, who had a school there. When Valdés was 25 he married a Cordovan, Doña Isabel Martínez de Morales, who also painted. After seven years, and a working trip to Carmona in 1653, he moved back to the rich cultural center of Seville, whose religious and charitable institutions gave him abundant employment.

On January 11, 1660, Seville's most respected painters and sculptors launched their public academy of drawing, and Valdés, one of the founders, was elected to manage its finances. He gave up this position after ten months, and although he was renominated in 1663, his excitable personality, and the disputes that always centered around him, did not allow him to continue in the office. On November 25 he was given the presidency as a peace offering. This he held for three years, acquiring a reputation for aggressive pride. Further quarrels caused him to resign on October 30, 1666, and he never entered the academy again, even when its new constitution was being signed ten years later.

Between Valdés and Bartolomé Murillo, the first president of the Seville Academy, there was particular jealousy. Murillo's discreet vision was the antithesis of Valdés' art, which matched his erratic character and his extraordinary energy. He had been able from the start to paint faster than his teacher Castillo, and explored, without preliminary studies, the dramatic, the violent, and the macabre. This technique was reinforced by his study of Flemish paintings, especially those of Rubens and van Dyck, which were popularized and copied in contemporary Spain. The resulting color, light, and movement produced a realism so effective that when his two allegories, *Death* and *Vanity*, were put up in the newly reconstructed church of the Hospital de La Caridad in 1672, the dead and decaying bodies which he had painted provoked Murillo to exlaim: "My good man, it's just as if one had to hold one's nose."

The hospital confraternity paid 5,740 *reales* for these pictures, his masterpieces, and two years later asked Valdés to make a title page for their inventory of furniture, pictures, and jewels. He made a graceful pen and watercolor drawing. At the end of the same year, 1674, he visited Madrid, saw everything, and attended all the gatherings—the small academies—which the famous masters held in the evenings in their own houses.

In 1682 Murillo died, and Valdés became the most highly esteemed painter in Seville. However, his work was already degenerating and his son Lucas often had to help him. He was attacked by a paralysis from which he died in 1691.

E. du G. Trapier Valdés Leal New York, 1956

HIS WORKS INCLUDE

Attack of the Saracens on the Convent of St. Francis, about 1654
Seville, Mus. Provincial de B. A.

The Assumption of Elias, 1658
Cordova, Carmelite Convent

The Immaculate Conception with Two Donors, 1661
London, N. G.

The Triumph of Death, 1672
Seville, Hospital de La Caridad

Allegory of Vanity, 1672
Seville, Hospital de La Caridad

See also page 248

Christ with the Scribes, 1686
Madrid, Prado

Courtier and great court painter of subtlety and brilliance

Diego Velázquez was born in Seville in 1599, and baptized there in June of that year. His father, Juan Rodríguez de Silva, came from a Portuguese family established in Seville only two generations before. The family of his mother, Jerónima de Velázquez, was a distinguished one, and it was their name which Velázquez invariably used in his signature. His parents were not wealthy, but they took great care with his education. First he studied Latin and philosophy, and then painting with the elder Francisco Herrera. In spite of this master's excellent, forceful teaching, Velázquez was soon moved to Francisco Pacheco's studio, where he was apprenticed for a trial period of nine months, and then, at the age of 12, for a further five years. Pacheco provided him with bed, board, and a sound set of rules by which to paint. Pacheco was just back from a visit to El Greco in Toledo, and the sight of the clay figures which the old painter used as models for his pictures had impressed him with the importance of rendering volume convincingly in painting. This emphasis he passed on to Velázquez, who learned the same lesson from Pacheco's classes in coloring statues, from a study of the sculpture of Juan Martínez Montañés, and from the pictures by Caravaggio that were beginning to reach Seville. His early works, such as *The Adoration of the Magi*, about 1619, show him to be influenced by Caravaggio in the use of light and shadow for throwing bodies into sharp relief. Then, like Caravaggio and Montañés, Velázquez found

Self-portrait: from The Maids of
Honor, about 1656
Madrid, Prado

The Topers, 1628
Madrid, Prado

Aesop, about 1640
Madrid, Prado

the basis for his mature style in a vivid feeling for the real and close study of nature.

Pacheco was a weak painter without the capacity to practice what he taught, but he was able to recognize the brilliant talent and good character of his pupil. He insisted on marrying the 19-year-old Velázquez to his daughter, Juana de Miranda. In 1617 Velázquez had already passed the entrance examination for the Seville Guild of St. Luke, and he was able to set up as a practicing master in the town.

In 1622 Velázquez made a short visit to Madrid and introduced himself at the court with a portrait of the poet Luis de Gongora y Argote. The king's minister, the Count-Duke Olivares, sent for him in April of the next year. He was an immediate success with a publicly acclaimed portrait of Philip IV himself on horseback. In October he was engaged in the king's service, with the promise that he should be his only portraitist. He moved his family to Madrid and in token of a new and permanent friendship with the king took up a lifelong succession of palace duties, many of which had nothing to do with his profession as a painter. Velázquez preserved his dignity and his identity, and perfected his art in court portraits and historical pictures along the lines on which he had begun in religious pictures, still-lifes, and domestic scenes.

Talks with the much-traveled Rubens, who often came to visit Velázquez when he was in Madrid from 1628 to 1629, made him want to see Italy; in July, 1629,

Don Baltasar Carlos on Horseback, about 1634
Madrid, Prado

The Lady with a Fan, 1640
London, Wallace Coll.

Infanta Margareta Theresa, about 1657
Vienna, Kunsthist. Mus.

211

The Buffoon Don Sebastían de Mora,
about 1648
Madrid, Prado

as a fair exchange for his picture of the year before, *The Topers*, the king sent him on royal business to all the Italian provinces. First, in Venice, he studied Jacopo Tintoretto, Paolo Veronese, and other masters of color and light. In the next year, going by way of Ferrara to Rome, he made copies of the Michelangelos and the Raphaels in the Vatican; and in Naples toward the end of the year he was shown over the city by José de Ribera, as devoted an admirer of Caravaggio as Velázquez himself had been. Everywhere he bought pictures for the king's collections, and at the beginning of 1631 he returned to Madrid.

Velázquez also brought back the memory of some of the compositions of Michelangelo and Raphael. *The Spinners*, for example, one of his last pictures, has been shown to be a transposition of the layout of Michelangelo's Sistine Chapel ceiling. It was, however, in Venice and in the Venice-inspired paintings of El Greco that Velázquez discovered the new dimension in which he now painted. Working with exquisite color harmonies, he spattered his compositions with a broken light which never destroyed their realism but softened their rigidity, and successfully superimposed on them the pattern of a personal vision, a suggestion of the ideal. Modeling was as important to him as before, but he achieved it now by heightening rather than deepening the picture surface so that direct contrasts of shadow with light were no longer necessary.

Late in 1648, 20 years after his first journey abroad, the king again sent Velázquez to Italy to buy pictures. Back in Madrid within three years, he began his greatest works, among them *The Maids of Honor (Las Meninas)*, which were so subtle in their combination of the real and the ideal that they became the inspiration of Goya, and later of the Impressionists.

Velázquez was a perfectionist. There are many *pentimenti* or "second thoughts" in his work, and his total production, though he had numerous assistants, was

Cupid: from The Toilet of Venus
before 1651   *London, N. G.*

The Spinners (detail) about 1657
Madrid, Prado

small. Moreover, it was increasingly hampered by his court duties. In 1652 he was made grand chamberlain to the palace, and in 1659 the king appealed to the pope for a dispensation that would allow his favorite artist to become a member of the Order of Santiago. On November 28, 1659, Velázquez was finally received into the order. Next year, when the court removed temporarily to the northern frontier of Spain to escort the Infanta María Theresa to meet her future husband, King Louis XIV of France, the entire arrangements for the lodgings en route and the ceremonial on the Isle of Pheasants were left in Velázquez's hands. He set out with a carpenter and sweepers two weeks ahead of the rest of the party, but he was a sick man, and died of fever and strain on August 6, 1660, not much more than a month after his return to Madrid.

E. du G. Trapier Velázquez New York, 1948
X. de Salas Velázquez London, 1962
J. López-Rey Velázquez: A Catalogue Raisonné of his Oeuvre London, 1963

HIS WORKS INCLUDE

The Adoration of the Magi, about 1619
Madrid, Prado

The Poet Luis de Gongora y Argote
1622
Boston, Mass., Mus. of Fine Arts

The Topers, 1628
Madrid, Prado

Vulcan's Forge, 1630
Madrid, Prado

Queen Mariana, 1652-53
Madrid, Prado

The Christ of S. Plácido
Madrid, Prado

See also pages 237, 238, 239, 240, 241, 261, 264

HERNANDO YÁÑEZ DE LA ALMEDINA   active to about 1536

A follower of Leonardo da Vinci

Hernando Yáñez was born in the town of Almedina in the region of La Mancha. He began by painting in the mixed Spanish-Flemish style then current in Spain. However, before long he went to work in Florence with Leonardo da Vinci and visited Venice. Another young painter from La Mancha, Hernando de Llanos, was also working with Leonardo. In 1505, Leonardo was painting *The Battle of Anghiari* for the Palazzo Vecchio in Florence, and one of the Hernandos was his assistant.

Both returned to Spain inspired by Leonardo, and became partners in 1506. On March 1, 1507, they were commissioned to paint new shutters for a silver altarpiece for Valencia Cathedral. The work, 12 scenes from *The Life of The Virgin*, took three years to complete. The figures have Leonardesque faces, and show the *sfumato* and *chiaroscuro* technique typical of Leonardo's followers, and of another Florentine, Piero di Cosimo.

Yáñez's pungent, still Spanish genius could present sacred themes in new and realistic contexts; his *Pentecost* took place out of doors, and classical backgrounds were varied with contemporary Valencian country and townscape. Character, as seen in the conscious restraint of the young Virgin in *The Presentation*, was sensitively drawn. This naturalistic eye accounted for Yáñez's excellence in genre, with everyday touches such as a still-life or a group of spectators perhaps more finely painted than the main subject of his picture.

Soon afterwards the two artists separated, and Yáñez worked in Barcelona. Later he went to Cuenca, where he painted in the cathedral from 1526 to 1531. He probably returned to Almedina for his last five years, and painted for churches there. His fame endured and inspired, in the next century, the dedication of an epigram from the great writer Francisco de Quevedo.

St. Catherine
Madrid, Prado

HIS WORKS INCLUDE

The Life of the Virgin, 1507-10
Valencia, Cath.

Altarpiece, 1526
Cuenca, Cath., Albornoz Chapel

The Madonna and Child with
St. Anne, St. Elizabeth, and St. John
the Baptist
Madrid, Prado

See also page 225

FRANCISCO GOYA
Francisco de Zurbarán
(copy of Self-portrait)
Paris, Louvre

F. ĐZVRBARAN.

FRANCISCO DE ZURBARÁN   1598-1664

A painter known for his mystical pictures

Francisco de Zurbarán was born into a peasant farmer family in the small town of
Fuente de Cantos, near Badajoz, in the region of Estremadura. When Zurbarán
was 12, it was discovered that he liked painting and he was sent to Seville. In the
painting school of Juan de Roelas he made extraordinary progress. When he left at
16, Zurbarán had already made an artistic reputation in the city, and was immediately taken on as an apprentice by an embroidery painter there, Pedro Díaz
de Villanueva. Two years with this master made him at 18 a mature and accomplished technician. At the same time he met Diego Velázquez, who was also an
apprentice in Seville. Like Velázquez he took the paintings of Caravaggio and José
de Ribera as his models. These influences endured; the placing of big patches of
light and shade, which he learned from the work of the two painters, was the appropriate vehicle for expressing a feeling for volume. From Juan Martínez Montañés, Caravaggio, and Ribera he also acquired the realism that was the basis of
his earlier style, and gave to the faces of *The Apostles*, for example, painted about
1623, the features of rough peasants. Zurbarán was not yet interested in the ideal.

St. Dorothy (detail) about 1650
Seville, Provincial Mus. de B. A.

The Miracle of St. Hugo, about 1633
Seville, Provincial Mus. de B. A.

In 1617, after visits to Valencia and Valladolid, Zurbarán returned to live for some years at Llerena, in his native Estremadura. There he married Beatriz de Morales. He made working trips to Seville from time to time, and a deputation was sent from the city council to beg him to make his permanent home there. In 1628 he did so, and was immediately showered with contracts.

Zurbarán's greatest and most characteristic period now began. He did not entirely abandon his earlier realism. *The Apotheosis of St. Thomas Aquinas* of 1631, for example, though larger than life size, is a portrait of the prebendary of the college church for which it was painted; his female saints were often portraits of young ladies of Seville. He always created simple compositions consisting of a few figures in solemn and natural attitudes. It was this solemn, even mystical aspect of Zurbarán's personality, his vision rather than his means of expression, that came to the fore. In 1628 an order from the Seville Convent of La Merced for a series of pictures on the life of the recently canonized St. Peter Nolasco gave him the opening he needed: he now became the painter of the monastic life of asceticism and of ecstasies. He himself as a layman was consecrated a tertiary of St. Francis.

In 1629 there were protests by Alonso Cano and other rival artists when the council nominated Zurbarán as city painter of Seville. Five years later Philip IV invited him to Madrid to paint a series of pictures for his new palace, the Buen Retiro. He was appointed king's painter.

In 1639 Zurbarán's second wife died. Though he remarried he never recovered the equilibrium with which he had painted masterpieces for the religious houses of Seville, Jerez, and Guadalupe. For 25 years he lived and worked in Seville and Madrid, but it was possibly Murillo's success in Seville, and a vain attempt to keep up with him by oversentimentalizing, that caused the decline of Zurbarán's art.

M. S. Soria   The Paintings of Zurbarán   London and New York, 1955

The Young Virgin
New York, Met. Mus., Fletcher Fund

St. Luis Beltran, 1650
Seville, Provincial Mus. de B. A.

St. Margaret, about 1635
London, N. G.

215

FERRER BASSA The Madonna Enthroned, 1345-46 *fresco secco* $50 \times 39\frac{3}{4}$ *in.*
Pedralbes, Spain, Convent of the Nuns of the Order of St. Clare, St. Michael's Chapel

LUIS BORRASSÁ   The Resurrection (detail): from the Altar of St. Creus, before 1414
tempera on panel
Barcelona, Museum of Catalan Art

LUIS DALMÁU The Madonna of the Councilors, 1443-45 *tempera and oil on panel*
Barcelona, Museum of Catalan Art

JACOMART S. Ildefonso and Alfonso de Borja, 1451-55 *tempera on panel*
Valencia, College of Játiva

JAIME HUGUET   The Adoration of the Magi: from the Altar of the Condestable of Portugal
about 1465   *tempera on panel   61¾ × 39⅜ in.*
Barcelona, S. Agueda

FERNANDO GALLEGO The Madonna of the Rose, about 1475 *oil on panel* *46½ × 27 in.*
Salamanca, Museo Diocesano

PEDRO BERRUGUETE St. Peter Martyr and the Crucifix, about 1500
oil on panel 51⅜ × 33⅞ *in.*
Madrid, Prado

RODRIGO DE OSONA The Madonna with the Montesa Knight, 1476-84 *oil on panel* 40⅜ × 37¾ *in.*
Madrid, Prado

224

HERNANDO YAÑEZ DE LA ALMEDINA The Adoration of the Shepherds, 1507 *oil on panel 76¾ × 89¾ in.*
Valencia, Cathedral

PEDRO MACHUCA The Deposition, after 1520 *oil on panel* 55½ × 50⅜ *in.*
Madrid, Prado

JUAN DE JUANES The Last Supper *oil on panel* $45\frac{5}{8} \times 75\frac{1}{4}$ *in.*
Madrid, Prado

LUIS DE MORALES The Madonna and Child *oil on panel 33⅜ × 25¼ in.*
Madrid, Prado

EL GRECO   The Holy Trinity, 1577-79   *oil on canvas*   118⅛ × 70½ *in.*
Madrid, Prado

EL GRECO The Martyrdom of St. Maurice and the Theban Legion (detail), 1580-82   *oil on canvas   176⅜ × 118½ in.*
near Madrid, The Escorial

EL GRECO   The Burial of Count Orgaz, 1586-88   *oil on canvas*   *191⅞ × 141¾ in.*
Toledo, S. Tomé

EL GRECO   Cardinal Don Fernando Niño de Guevara, about 1600   *oil on canvas* $67\frac{1}{4} \times 42\frac{1}{2}$ *in.*
New York, Metropolitan Museum of Art

EL GRECO Laocoön (detail), about 1610-1614 *oil on canvas* 55⅞×76 *in.*
Washington, D. C., National Gallery of Art, Kress Collection

JOSÉ DE RIBERA The Martyrdom of St. Bartholomew, 1630 (?) *oil on canvas 92⅛ × 92⅛ in.*
Madrid, Prado

JOSÉ DE RIBERA The Holy Trinity, 1636 *oil on canvas 89 × 71¼ in.*
Madrid, Prado

JOSÉ DE RIBERA St. Agnes in Prison, 1641 *oil on canvas* $79\frac{1}{4} \times 59\frac{7}{8}$ *in.*
Dresden, Gemäldegalerie

DIEGO VELÁZQUEZ Old Woman Frying Eggs, about 1618 *oil on canvas 39 × 46 in.*
Edinburgh, National Gallery of Scotland

DIEGO VELÁZQUEZ   The Surrender of Breda, 1635   *oil on canvas   121⅛ × 144¾ in.*
Madrid, Prado

DIEGO VELÁZQUEZ   The Maids of Honor, about 1656   *oil on canvas*   125¼ × 108⅞ *in.*
Madrid, Prado

DIEGO VELÁZQUEZ   Pope Innocent X, 1650   *oil on canvas*   55⅛ × 47¼ *in.*
Rome, Doria Pamphili Palace

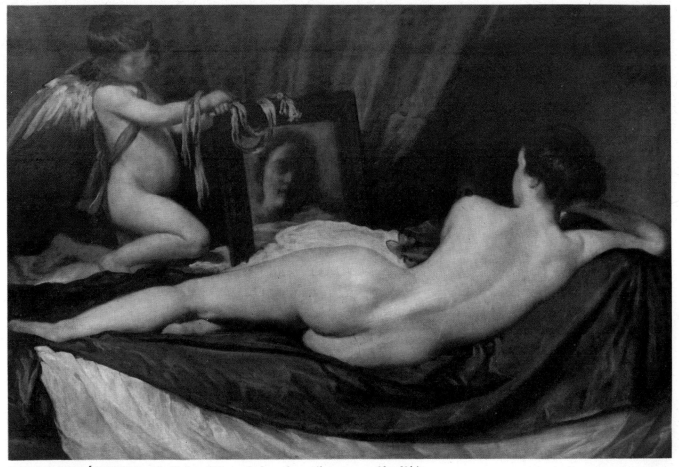

DIEGO VELÁZQUEZ   The Toilet of Venus, before 1651   *oil on canvas   48¼×68¼ in.*
London, National Gallery

FRANCISCO DE ZURBARÁN The Death of S. Bonaventura, about 1629 *oil on canvas 98¾ × 88⅝ in.*
Paris, Louvre

FRANCISCO DE ZURBARÁN The Immaculate Conception, about 1632 *oil on canvas*
Barcelona, Museum of Catalan Art

FRANCISCO DE ZURBARÁN The Annunciation, about 1658   *oil on canvas* $83\frac{3}{4} \times 123\frac{1}{2}$ *in.*
Philadelphia, Pa., Museum of Art, Wilstach Collection

ALONSO CANO The Immaculate Conception, 1650 *oil on canvas* *72 × 44¼ in.*
Vitoria, Spain, Museo Provincial de Bellas Artes

BARTOLOMÉ ESTEBAN MURILLO A Girl and her Duenna, about 1665-75 *oil on canvas* $49\frac{5}{8} \times 41\frac{3}{4}$ *in.*
Washington, D. C., National Gallery of Art, Widener Collection

BARTOLOMÉ ESTEBAN MURILLO   The Dream of the Patrician: from The Foundation of S. Maria Maggiore, about 1665
oil on canvas   91⅜ × 205½ in.
Madrid, Prado

JUAN DE VALDÉS LEAL The Temptation of St. Jerome, 1657 *oil on canvas* $87\frac{3}{8} \times 97\frac{1}{4}$ *in.*
Seville, Museo Provincial de Bellas Artes

CLAUDIO COELLO   The Madonna and Child and the Theological Virtues, 1669   *oil on canvas* $91\frac{3}{8} \times 107\frac{7}{8}$ *in.*
Madrid, Prado

LUIS EGIDIO MELÉNDEZ Still-life, 1772 *oil on canvas* *16½ × 24⅜ in.*
Madrid, Prado

FRANCISCO GOYA The Parasol, 1777 *oil on canvas 41 × 60 in.*
Madrid, Prado

FRANCISCO GOYA The Countess del Carpio, Marchioness of Solana, 1791-95
oil on canvas   72 × 48¾ in.
Paris, Louvre, De Besteigui Collection

FRANCISCO GOYA   The Family of Charles IV, 1800   *oil on canvas   110 × 132 in.*
Madrid, Prado

FRANCISCO GOYA   The Second of May 1808, painted 1814 *oil on canvas 105 × 136 in.*
Madrid, Prado

FRANCISCO GOYA Don Juan Bautista de Muquiro, 1827 *oil on canvas* 40¼ × 33⅜ *in.*
Madrid, Prado

EDUARDO ROSALES The Death of Lucretia, 1871 *oil on canvas* $100\frac{3}{8} \times 134\frac{1}{8}$ *in.*
Madrid, Museo Nacional de Arte Moderno

Drawings

PEDRO DE CAMPAÑA The Deposition *pen and ink* $7\frac{7}{8} \times 4\frac{3}{4}$ *in.*
Madrid, Biblioteca Nacional

ALONSO BERRUGUETE The Transfiguration *red chalk* $16\frac{1}{4} \times 9\frac{1}{4}$ *in.*
Florence, Uffizi

GASPAR BECERRA   Design for the Altar of the Descalzas Reales, 1563
pen and ink   34¼ × 19⅝ in.
Madrid, Biblioteca Nacional

EL GRECO St. John the Evangelist, 1577 *pen and ink and pencil 9⅞ × 5⅞ in.*
Madrid, Biblioteca Nacional

DIEGO VELÁZQUEZ   View of Granada   *pen and wash* $7\frac{1}{8} \times 12\frac{1}{4}$ *in.*
Madrid, Biblioteca Nacional

FRANCISCO PACHECO   Christ in the Wilderness Served by Angels, 1615
pen and wash $8\frac{5}{8} \times 10\frac{5}{8}$ *in.*   *Barcelona, Museum of Art*

FRANCISCO RIBALTA St. John the Baptist *pen and ink* 9¼ × 5¼ *in.*
Madrid, Prado

JOSÉ DE RIBERA Acrobats
Madrid, Real Academia de San Fernando

DIEGO VELÁZQUEZ   Portrait of a Woman, about 1623   *black pencil* $5\frac{7}{8} \times 4\frac{3}{4}$ *in.*
Madrid, Biblioteca Nacional

JERÓNIMO JACINTO DE ESPINOSA The Annunciation *pen and wash* $12\frac{7}{8} \times 8\frac{7}{8}$ *in.*
Princeton University, Princeton, N.J., Art Museum

ALONSO CANO   The Madonna of the Angels   *pen and brown wash* $5\frac{1}{2} \times 10\frac{1}{4}$ *in.*
Madrid, Prado

ALONSO CANO Design for a Porch *pen*
Madrid, collection Duke of Fernán Nuñez

FRANCISCO CAMILO St. Francis of Paola, 1673
pen and wash $7\frac{7}{8} \times 5\frac{7}{8}$ *in.*
Madrid, Prado

ANTONIO DEL CASTILLO Head of a Boy
pen and wash $9\frac{7}{8} \times 6\frac{1}{2}$ *in.*
Madrid, Prado

SEBASTIÁN DE HERRERA BARNUEVO Portrait of a Man *pencil* 9⅞ × 7⅞ *in.*
Florence, Uffizi

JUAN CARREÑO DE MIRANDA St. Anthony, 1656
pen and wash $9\frac{3}{8} \times 7\frac{1}{4}$ *in.*
Madrid, Prado

CLAUDIO COELLO Kneeling Woman *pencil* $14\frac{5}{8} \times 10\frac{5}{8}$ *in.*
Madrid, Prado

LUIS PARET Y ALCAZÁR   Maria Louisa of Parma, 1766-77
pen and wash   9⅞ × 7⅞ in.
London, British Museum

CLAUDIO COELLO   Flora (study for a ceiling)
pen and wash   9⅞ × 6½ in.
Madrid, Prado

Nada nos ynporta

FRANCISCO GOYA Couple Seated, after 1800 *sepia wash* 8⅛ × 5⅝ *in.*
Madrid, Prado

Sculpture

UNKNOWN SCULPTOR   Queen Beatrice? (detail) about 1260
marble
Burgos, Cathedral

JAIME CASTAYLS St. Charlemagne,
14th century *alabaster*
Gerona, Cathedral

GUILLERMO SAGRERA St. Peter, about 1422
stone $68\frac{7}{8} \times 15\frac{3}{4}$ *in.*
Palma de Mallorca, Cathedral

GIL DE SILOE Don Juan de Padilla: from his tomb, 1500-1503
alabaster 25¼ × 13¼ in.
Burgos, Museo Arqueológico

BARTOLOMÉ ORDÓÑEZ
St. Eulalia before the Roman Prefect, 1517-20 *marble relief*
Barcelona, Cathedral

ALONSO BERRUGUETE Abraham and Isaac, 1527-32
painted and gilded wood
Valladolid, Museo Nacional de Escultura Religiosa

ALONSO BERRUGUETE Eve, 1539-41 *wood relief*
Toledo, Cathedral

JUAN DE JUNI The Virgin of Sorrows, 1550   *approximately life size*
Valladolid, Museo Nacional de Escultura Religiosa

JUAN DE JUNI The Burial of Christ, 1571 *painted and gilded wood*
Segovia, Cathedral

POMPEO LEONI   Philip II and his Family: from the Tomb of Philip II, 1598-1600   *gilded bronze   66⅞ × 138¼ in.*
near Madrid, The Escorial

EL GRECO The Risen Christ, 1595-98
painted wood   height 17¾ in.
Toledo, Hospital de Tavera

GREGORIO FERNÁNDEZ Pietà, 1617
Valladolid, Museo Nacional de Escultura Religiosa

JUAN MARTÍNEZ MONTAÑÉS
The Adoration of the Shepherds (detail) 1610-13
painted wood   47 × 79 in.
Santiponce, Monastery of S. Isidro del Campo

JUAN DE MESA   The Christ of Love, 1618
painted wood
Seville, S. Salvador

ALONSO CANO The Child Jesus of the Passion
painted wood   height 27⅜ in.
Madrid, Cofradia de los Navarros

PEDRO DE MENA St. Francis of Assisi, 1663
painted wood
Toledo, Cathedral

JOSÉ DE MORA   The Virgin of Solitude, 1671
painted wood
Granada, S. Ana

NARCISO TOMÉ   The Madonna and Child: from the
Transparente, 1721-32   *painted wood*
Toledo, Cathedral

286

FRANCISCO SALZILLO St. Jerome, 1755 *painted wood* $63\frac{3}{4} \times 51\frac{1}{8}$ *in.*
Murcia, Museo Salzillo

DAMIÁN CAMPENY The Dead Lucretia, 1834 *carrara marble* $59\frac{3}{4} \times 25$ *in.*
Barcelona, Real Academia de Bellas Artes de San Jorge

a

b

Influences and Developments

Architecture Reveals the History of Spain

The development of architecture in Spain from the 13th to the 18th centuries was largely determined by the impact of a succession of imported styles. The early Moorish influence is seen in the motifs on the castle of Manzanares el Real (a). During the middle of the 13th century the French High Gothic style invaded Spain, and found an early expression in the large cathedral of León (b), modeled on the cathedral of Amiens with its elaborate tracery and beautiful stained-glass windows. The last Gothic cathedral, Segovia (c), was not completed until the 16th century, when contemporary buildings were being designed in the Renaissance style.

Although the basic structures of many 16th-century buildings were in the imported Renaissance style, the ornamentation on the façades formed a distinctly Spanish style called Plateresque. The style resulted from a fusion of Gothic, Moorish, and Renaissance motifs, executed with an elegance and delicacy reminiscent of silversmiths' work. Obelisks and palmettes replaced pinnacles and Gothic floral ornament. The medallions and armorial bearings on the façade of Salamanca University (d) are typically Plateresque.

Emperor Charles V preferred Italianate simplicity to Plateresque flourishes. Machuca's design for his palace (e) displays a gravity of line and somber tone typical of a contemporary Roman palace. The religious interpretation of Italianate

c

d

e

a The Castle: façade, after 1212
near Madrid, Manzanares el Real

b The Cathedral, about 1250-1305
yellow limestone
León

c The Cathedral, 1522-27
Segovia

d The University: façade, about 1530
brown sandstone
Salamanca

e Pedro Machuca
Palace of Charles V: façade,
begun 1526
Granada

289

forms is seen in the classical white pillars of the interior of Granada Cathedral (f). This classical tendency culminated in the art of Juan Herrera, who designed the Monastery of the Escorial for Philip II (g). It was the most representative work of Hapsburg Spain with its severe style and huge proportions. In the 17th and 18th centuries Italian Baroque succeeded in reaction to Herrera's purism. The extraordinary façade of Santiago de Compostela Cathedral (h), a work of Casas y Novoa, epitomized the fantasies of the Spanish imagination.

In the last third of the 18th century the transition from Hapsburg to Bourbon resulted in the adoption of French and Italian forms. Italian-inspired Neoclassicism found a fine exponent in Cabezas and Rodríguez, who were partially responsible for the Church of S. Francisco el Grande, Madrid (i), while an interpretation of French Rococo is seen in the Palace of the Marqués de Dos Aguas, Valencia (j).

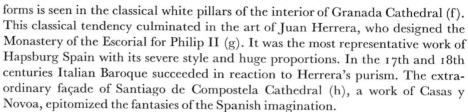

f

g

h

i

j

Christian Spain: Inside her Churches

Spanish churches have always been characterized by the variety and richness of their liturgical trappings. High altars served as a means for Spanish craftsmen to document their techniques. The Gothic and Renaissance sculptors' delicately carved reliefs and idealized figures were primarily Flemish-inspired (a, b).

Under the influence of the Italian Baroque, high altars became heavy and over-decorated. José de Churriguera's high altar of S. Esteban, Salamanca (c) is a unique spatial exploration, massive ornamentation filling the chancel right up to the dome. The Churrigueresque style reached its apogee when the decorative elements completely swamped the underlying structure. For example, the pilasters in the sacristy of the Carthusian Monastery in Granada (d), teeming with broken pediments, present a strong contrast to their classical predecessors.

Iron grills (*rejas*) were widely employed in Spanish churches to divide the space and to decorate the ensemble, allowing visibility at the same time. Some of the best examples are in Cuenca Cathedral (e).

a

b

c

d

e

a Gregorio Fernández
High Altar (detail)
Seville, Cathedral

b Gil de Siloe
Retable (detail)
Burgos, Carthusian Monastery

c José de Churriguera
High Altar, 1693
Salamanca, S. Esteban

d Interior of Sacristy, 1713-47
Granada, Carthusian Monastery

e View of Chapel with grill (*reja*)
Cuenca, Cathedral

17th and 18th-Century Interiors: Destined to house Great Masterpieces

Spanish painting flourished under the patronage of the church in the 17th century. The monasteries' white-washed walls and sturdy furniture were familiar backgrounds for paintings such as those of Zurbarán and Ricci (a). In the 17th century, artists also found willing patrons among the aristocracy. Velázquez's *Maids of Honor* sets a trend for family portraits in domestic settings; for example, *The Portrait of the Family of Ambassador Lerche* (b). The figures took precedence over the interiors, which were merely functional backgrounds. During the Baroque era, furnishings became more decorative with the sitter often eclipsed by the surroundings. Queen Mariana sitting at her writing desk is almost overshadowed by the lush paintings and mirrors on the wall of the Alcázar (c).

The change of dynasty ushered in a complete change of taste. Where once family portraits decorated the walls of fashionable salons, now late Baroque and French Rococo motifs (d) predominated, and sometimes covered the floors, ceilings and furnishings, as well as the walls. Tapestries in a frivolous style similar to that of Fragonard and Watteau were sometimes chosen to complement the sumptuous furnishings (e).

Rococo became unfashionable in the late 18th century and was replaced by refined neoclassical designs and colors.

a

b

c

d

e

The Influence of the Moors

Moslem art flourished in Spain from the 8th to the 15th century. It found its fullest expression in architecture—in hundreds of mosques, synagogues (Spanish Jews adopted Moorish architecture for their places of worship), palaces, baths, towers, and city gates. These structures were decorated with mosaics and plastic forms mostly derived from Byzantine and Visigothic art. The oldest and largest Moorish monument is the mosque at Cordova (a) with its forest of red and white horseshoe-shaped arches in the interior.

Moorish art had penetrated so deeply into the society that, even after the conquest of Granada, it persisted under Christian rule. Moorish and Christian currents, with the former given more prominence, mingled to form the Mudéjar style. The synagogue of S. Maria la Blanca (converted to a Christian church in 1405) is an example of this fusion. Moorish elements are seen in the interior (b).

The most beautiful Moorish palace, the Alhambra, has arches with an arabesque pattern delicately carved and strikingly set against the simple, low-pitched roofs in the Patio of the Lions (c). These roofs appear again on the Moorish summer palace, the Generalife (d), which looks down on a magnificent garden.

In the sphere of the applied arts the Moorish influence had its greatest impact. Under the patronage of the Spanish aristocracy, Maníses, near Valencia became a center that produced luster ware (e) until the 18th century.

a Interior of Mosque, begun 785
*marble, porphyry, jasper,
and breccia columns
Cordova, La Mezquita*

b Synagogue of S. María la Blanca,
interior, 12th or 13th century
*stucco
Toledo*

c Patio of the Lions, begun 1377
*wood and plaster walls with
ivory decoration
Granada, Alhambra*

d View of the Garden, before 1494
Granada, Generalife

e Valencian dish with the arms of
the Counts of Ribarcorza and
Prades of the House of Aragón,
about 1420
*luster ware   18 in. diameter
London, British Museum*

a

b

c

d

e

Colonial Architecture

Colonial art grew out of the union of two very different civilizations; the pre-Columbian cultures which existed in Mexico, Guatemala, Colombia, Ecuador, Peru, and Bolivia, and the styles imported from the mother country.

Hispano-American buildings were usually simple in structure, due to the absence of virtuoso architects and the severe climatic conditions (earthquakes, volcanic eruptions, and hurricanes). During the late 16th century and early 17th century, the architecture was mainly a mixture of classical structures and early Baroque ornamentations, such as the massive volutes on the Cathedral of Mexico City (a).

Later in the 17th century the ostentatiously elegant air of the Baroque spirit captured the colonial imagination. In Mexico, beautifully-colored tiles were used to decorate the simple façades (b). In Peru, a native style with retable façades evolved from Spanish Baroque forms and flourished from 1680 to 1730. Its motifs included twisted Corinthianesque capitals, giving a feeling of spirited abandon (c). The period from 1730 to 1780 was called the Ultra-Baroque, or the Mexican Churrigueresque. In Ecuador, both the Spanish and Italian Baroque were blended into the twisted colomns of the façade of La Compañía (d). In Mexico, however, the height of the *estípite* era is seen in the façade of the Church of S. Martín at Tepotzotlán (e). Another fusion of styles, this time the Moorish and European (neo-Mudéjar), is seen in the 18th-century façade of the Archbishop's Palace in Lima (f) with its large carved wooden balconies (*miradores*).

a The Cathedral, about 1573-1656
basalt and gray sandstone
Mexico City

b Façade, after 1696-before 1730
tile
Tonantzintla, Mexico, Church of
S. María

c Pulpit (detail) about 1680-95
wood
Cuzco, Peru, S. Blás Church

d Façade, begun 1722
Quito, Ecuador, La Compañiá

e Façade, 1760-62
Tepotzotlán, Mexico, S. Martín

f Façade, 18th century,
reconstructed in 1929
Lima, Peru, The Archbishop's Palace

g Façade, 1728
Potosí, Bolivia, S. Lorenzo

h Retable, 1775
S. Luis Potosí, Mexico, Cathedral

a

b

The culmination of Hispano-American art is thought to be the Church of S. Lorenzo, Potosí, Bolivia (g). Here, the *mestizo* carver's stone creations paralleled the
wood carver's works in Spain. Finally, the colonial style of the late 18th century
degenerated into late Baroque overdecoration and Rococo glitter, as seen in a
Mexican retable (h).

c

d

e

f

g

h

The Applied Arts

The applied arts have always been widely cultivated in Spain. Her unique heritage of both Moslem and European idioms produced unusually beautiful designs. Decorated wooden cabinets personifying the fusion of Moslem and Renaissance motifs were made at Bargas in the 16th and 17th centuries. A type of wooden cabinet called *vargueño* (a combined writing desk and depository for valuables) with its intricate geometrical inlays worked by Moorish craftsmen, was a particular source of pride (a). Mudéjar-style rugs (b) were being woven in Cuenca and Alcaraz at the same time. Their Oriental motifs became the hallmarks of yet another industry in which Spain excelled.

Nor were European craftsmen absent from the Spanish heyday of the applied arts. A Spanish family of Flemish origin—the Arphes—made magnificent monstrances for processions in the style of the Italian Renaissance. The one at Toledo Cathedral (c) is most outstanding, with no less than 260 silver-gilt statuettes.

Later in the 18th century the perfection and richness of Spanish embroidery is seen in the dalmatic of Ferdinand VI (d). At the same time, encouraged by the Spanish court, other craftsmen were producing delightful polychromed porcelain figures in the factories of the Buen Retiro (e).

a

b

c

d

e

THE VOLUMES